English Idioms

Exercises
on Phrasal Verbs

Jennifer Seidl

Oxford University Press

Oxford University Press,
Walton Street, Oxford OX2 6DP

Oxford   New York   Toronto
Delhi   Bombay   Calcutta   Madras   Karachi
Petaling Jaya   Singapore   Hong Kong   Tokyo
Nairobi   Dar es Salaam   Cape Town
Melbourne   Auckland

and associated companies in
Berlin   Ibadan

Oxford and *Oxford English* are
trade marks of Oxford University Press.

ISBN 0 19 432786 8

First edition 1990
Fourth impression 1991

© Jennifer Seidl 1990

The publishers would like to thank the following for
permission to reproduce photographs: Richard and Sally
Greenhill, Relay Photos, Singapore Airlines, The Sunday
Times Magazine (London) and Philip Oakley.

Cartoons reproduced by permission of Punch.

Illustrated by: Jane Gedye
                Martin Lonsdale, Hardlines

The publishers would like to thank the following for
their permission to use adapted extracts from copyright
material in Part II: H Bauer Publishing for extracts
from *Bella* magazine in exercises 21 and 45, *best*
magazine for material written by Tessa Harris, Margaret
Jones, Robin Corry and Michael van Straten used in
exercises 28, 33, 38 and 40, *Chat* magazine for the
second article in exercise 40, Ladybird Books Ltd for
puzzles from *The Ladybird Book of Puzzles* in exercise 24,
The Sunday Times Magazine (London) and Nick
Smurthwaite for the article in exercise 46, Usborne
Publishing Ltd for extracts from *The Usborne Book of
Puzzles* in exercises 23 and 24 and Writers House Inc
for the extract from *Never Work for a Jerk* by Patricia
King in exercise 34.

Set by Wyvern Typesetting Ltd, Bristol
Printed in Hong Kong

Contents

Introduction

About this book

This book has been written especially for students of English who wish to improve their understanding and active use of phrasal verbs. It is suitable for all learners from an intermediate level upwards, either as a first book on phrasal verbs or as a revision and practice book.

Exercises on Phrasal Verbs can be used in the classroom or for self-study. The contents are based on *English Idioms* (fifth edition, Oxford University Press 1988, by Seidl and McMordie) but the book is complete in itself and can be used independently.

Content and organization

The book describes, explains and exercises all types of phrasal verb in a lively, innovative way. The book has two parts. Part I is essentially a reference and demonstration section. It explains systematically six structural types of phrasal verb plus nominalized forms and demonstrates clearly how they work. Part I also includes exercises which concentrate on familiarizing the student with the form and meaning of common phrasal verbs. Part II is a varied section of exercises introducing a larger number of phrasal verbs.

Approach

Part II introduces a new approach to the teaching and exercising of phrasal verbs. Exercises are based on a communicative approach to language learning. Phrasal verbs are not dealt with in unconnected sets of mechanical sentences but are presented for study and practice in natural contexts, within real language situations, for example in the form of letters, magazine articles, quizzes, puzzles, horoscopes, etc. Several texts used are authentic or have been adapted from authentic written material. Other exercises make use of the student's own knowledge, experience, and opinions. This feature makes the book particularly interesting for classroom use and for pair work or group work, as several of the exercises promote discussion or present a problem-solving challenge.

How to use this book

For readers wishing to cover the subject of phrasal verbs thoroughly, it would be desirable to work through the book from beginning to end. Advanced learners who are already acquainted with phrasal verb structures may wish to concentrate on the exercises of Part II, using Part I for reference. In either case, it is advisable to tackle the exercises of Part I before progressing to Part II.

Part II can be worked through from beginning to end or exercises can be chosen in any order. The early exercises concentrate on one phrasal verb only; the last ones contain up to 20 phrasal verbs. Students can check their progress by doing the test exercises, which do not contain reference material. For a full description of the exercises and advice on how to use them, see the introduction to Part II on page 34.

English Idioms

With a few exceptions, the phrasal verbs used in this book are to be found in chapter 6 (pages 101–154) of *English Idioms* (fifth edition, Oxford University Press 1988), with full explanations and examples.

If a phrasal verb has additional meanings to those given here which can be found in *English Idioms*, the page reference is given in brackets, e.g. (EI 121).

Alternative phrasal verbs with the same meaning are also indicated with the page reference from *English Idioms*.

PART I What are phrasal verbs?

In this book *phrasal verb* is a general term for all combinations of *verb+adverbial particle* and/or *preposition*. Some examples are **fall through, pack something in, put up with someone/ something.**

Meaning

A phrasal verb can have more than one meaning. Its meaning may be *non-idiomatic* or *idiomatic*. If the phrasal verb is idiomatic, it has a special meaning which we cannot easily guess from the meaning of the separate words.

For example, the non-idiomatic meaning of **fall through** is clear:

The ice was thin and Jimmy fell through.

i.e. he fell through the ice into the water. However, the idiomatic meaning of **fall through** bears no relationship to the individual words **fall** and **through**, as in:

Sue had plans to go to Africa, but they fell through.

Here, **fall+through** form an idiomatic phrasal verb with the meaning 'fail'.

Here is another example using the phrasal verb **pack something in**. In the following sentence it has a non-idiomatic meaning:

She opened her suitcase and packed all the clothes in.

However, in the sentence

She decided to pack her job in.

the individual meanings of **pack** and **in** do not convey the idiomatic meaning, which (here) is 'leave'. Because of this phrasal verbs have to be learnt and practised in their combinations.

As shown above, a phrasal verb can have a non-idiomatic

meaning and an idiomatic meaning. Some phrasal verbs have several idiomatic meanings, depending on the words that accompany them, i.e. their 'collocations'. For example, **take off**:

The aircraft/flight/pilot took off.
i.e. left the ground

The thief/boy/dog (people or animals) *took off.*
i.e. ran away in a hurry

Sales/the economy/the new product took off.
i.e. began to improve greatly, make a big profit

Structures

There are three basic combinations of verb, adverbial particle and preposition. These are:

Verb+particle
Verb+preposition
Verb+particle+preposition

In their *Oxford Dictionary of Current Idiomatic English*, A. P. Cowie and R. Mackin present these combinations in a system of patterns, three *intransitive* (i.e. there is no direct object) and three *transitive* (i.e. there is a direct object).

This gives us six patterns:

1 Intransitive+particle
   e.g. **slow down, get on, take off**

2 Intransitive+preposition
   e.g. **go off someone/something**
   count on someone/something

3 Intransitive+particle+preposition
   e.g. **put up with someone/something**
   come up against someone/something

4 Transitive+particle
   e.g. **pack something in**
   take someone off

5 Transitive+preposition
   e.g. **talk someone into something**
   turn someone off someone/something

6   Transitive+particle+preposition
    e.g. **put someone up to something**
        take someone up on something

someone and *something*

In the patterns above and throughout the book the words *someone* and *something* indicate where the direct object and/or the object of the preposition usually stand. This is important, as the meaning of some phrasal verbs depends on the presence and position of a direct or prepositional object. For example, compare:

see through something (pattern 2: intransitive with
                              prepositional object)
I saw through the plan. = I recognized the deception of the plan.

see something through (pattern 4: transitive with direct object)
I saw the plan through. = I persevered with the plan until it was
                                 completed.

someone and *something* also indicate that a particular phrasal verb has different meanings when used with a *person* and with a *thing*. Compare:

put someone off   = 1 distract someone or disturb someone's
                        concentration
                   = 2 keep someone waiting for a decision

put something off = postpone/delay something

set about someone = attack someone physically or with words

set about something = begin to do something

If there is no difference in meaning the slant (/) is used. For example **go off someone/something.**

1 Intransitive+particle

> **slow down**
> **get on**
> **take off**

This combination represents a large group of phrasal verbs. It is simple in structure and therefore one of the easiest groups to use.

Structure

A verb combines with a word such as *over, on, off, up, down, across, in*, etc. In this pattern these words, which can also function as prepositions, function as *adverbial particles* because they do not introduce a noun phrase or pronoun. Instead, they are used to change the meaning of a verb, independently of an object. The pattern is *intransitive*, i.e. there is no direct object.

Study these examples and their meanings.

Verb	Particle	Meaning
slow	down	decrease speed
get	on	have a good relationship
take	off	leave the ground

Stress

When the phrasal verb is in isolation, e.g. for learning purposes, the stress is always on the particle. Within a sentence the stress is also on the particle when the phrasal verb stands alone at the end of a sentence (or clause) as in the following:

The lorry slowed 'down and came to a halt.
Do Tom and the new man get 'on?
What time did the flight eventually take 'off?

In other cases, especially when an adverb follows the phrasal verb, the usual rules for sentence stress apply:

The lorry slowed down i'mmediately.
Tom and the new man get on 'well.
The flight took off later than 'scheduled.

Note: There is a relationship between some Pattern 1 and some Pattern 4 phrasal verbs. Some intransitive patterns can become transitive by the addition of a direct object:

Pattern 1   Pattern 4
slow down   **slow something down**
The driver slowed down. *The driver slowed the car down.*

Note however that the patterns are not always related in meaning, as with **take off, take something off** and **take someone off**:

Pattern 1: *The plane took off.* (It left the ground.)
Pattern 4: *He took his coat off.* (He removed his coat.)
Pattern 4: *She took Mrs Thatcher off.* (She imitated Mrs Thatcher.)

Now study these phrasal verbs, their meanings and the examples, then use them in the exercises following.

come along develop; progress. *How's your new book coming along?* (EI 112. Also **come on**, EI 112)

get on have a good relationship; live/work well together. *Do Tom and the new man get on?* (EI 120. Also **get along**, EI 119)

hold on wait. *Hold on until I fetch help!* (Also **hang on**, EI 125)

set off begin a journey. *We didn't set off until after ten o'clock.* (Also **set out**, EI 142)

slow down decrease speed. *The lorry slowed down and came to a halt.*

take off leave the ground. *What time did the flight eventually take off?* (EI 147)

Exercise 1

Complete the sentences with the correct particle.

▶ We set _____ at seven thirty and arrived here at lunch-time.
off

1 We're coming to a corner. You had better slow _____. ⟶

2 The plane took _____ on time.

3 If that's Jane on the telephone, ask her to hold _____.

4 When did you set _____ from Glasgow?

5 I like our new teacher. I hope we'll get _____ well.

6 Jill says her marketing report is coming _____ nicely. She should finish it by the end of the week.

Exercise 2

Replace the words in *italics* with a phrasal verb in its correct form.

▶ The book's upstairs. If you *wait*, I'll get it for you.
hold on

1 The plane to Rome was delayed because of fog. What time did it eventually *leave the ground*?

2 The roads are wet. If I were you I would *reduce speed*.

3 The work on the house is *progressing* very well. The bedrooms are all finished.

4 Ken's just gone out for a moment, but if you *wait* for a few minutes he'll be back.

5 The new manager is very pleasant. I'm sure we'll *work well together*.

6 We didn't *leave* until eleven o'clock, so we walked as fast as we could to get here on time.

Exercise 3

Complete the sentences with the most appropriate phrasal verb in its correct form.

▶ We arrived late at the airport, only twenty minutes before the flight was due to _____.
take off

1 If you _____ for a few minutes, I'll get the car and drive you home.

2 Ask Jack how the work on his new house is _____.

3 Our new neighbours seem very friendly. We should _____ well.

4 The flight was delayed. It _____ two hours later than scheduled.

5 It's a long drive to Bristol, so we ought to _____ as early as possible.

6 The car began to _____ and finally came to a halt.

2 Intransitive + preposition

> **count on someone/something**
> **go off someone/something**
> **look into something**

Structure

A verb combines with a word such as *over, off, on, across*, etc. In this pattern these words function as *prepositions* because they introduce a noun phrase or pronoun (the object of the preposition). This pattern is intransitive, i.e. there is no direct object. The words *someone* and *something* indicate the position and nature of the object of the preposition.

Study these examples and their meanings.

Verb	Preposition	Object of preposition	Meaning
count	**on**	**someone/something**	rely on or trust someone/something
go	**off**	**someone/something**	lose one's liking for someone/something
look	**into**	**something**	investigate or research something

Stress

No rule can be given here but the following guide-lines are useful. When the preposition has only one syllable, the verb is usually stressed. Note that the verb **go** can be an exception.

'count on someone/something
'go for something (EI 124)
go 'off someone/something

Note also that the verb **be** is *not* stressed:

be 'at someone
be 'with someone

When the preposition has two syllables, the preposition is usually stressed:

look 'into something

Now study these phrasal verbs, their meanings and the examples, then use them in the exercises following.

be at someone (informal) try to persuade someone in an unpleasant way; complain continually. *She's always at her husband to stop smoking.*

be with someone understand someone's explanation/argument/ thoughts, etc. *Can you repeat that, please? I'm not with you.* (EI 106)

count on someone rely on someone; trust someone to help. *You can always count on Ann to give you good advice.* (Also **bank on someone**, EI 105)

go off someone/something lose one's taste or liking for someone/something. *We've gone off camping holidays. We're going to a hotel this year.*

look into something investigate or research something. *The police are looking into the case very thoroughly.* (Also **go into something**, EI 124)

take after someone resemble someone. *Mary takes after her father in being strong-willed.*

Exercise 4

Complete the sentences with the correct preposition.

▷ Can we count _____ you to support our party in the election?
on

1 There has been a series of thefts at the school. The headmistress is going to look _____ the matter very thoroughly.
2 Eric takes _____ his father. They both play excellent golf.
3 Mum says Dad still hasn't repaired the leaking tap. Listen! She's _____ him again.

4   This is a difficult theory to grasp. Are you all still _____ me?
5   If you need help, remember that you can count _____ me at all times.
6   I enjoyed learning German at first, but I went _____ it when it got difficult.

Exercise 5

Replace the words in *italics* with a phrasal verb in its correct form.

▶   Steven *resembles* his father in being stubborn and hot-tempered.
    takes after

1   You promised us your help with the exhibition. Can we still *rely on* you?
2   When I explained a second time, David said he *understood* me. But I don't think he was being honest.
3   Jill *resembles* her Aunt Betsy in appearance. They're both dark-haired and have brown eyes.
4   'The Three Kings' used to be my favourite pop group, but I *lost my liking for* them when 'The Mad Four' became popular.
5   The insurance company has promised to *investigate* my complaint.
6   Sue must think I'm not satisfied with her work. I always seem to *be continually complaining about* her recently. I must apologize to her.

Exercise 6

Complete the sentences with the most appropriate phrasal verb in its correct form.

▶   The police are searching for a motive for the murder. They are _____ the victim's past very thoroughly.
    looking into

1   Jeff _____ me again this morning. He said I must give him back the money that he lent me by tomorrow.
2   Before we make a final decision, we'll have to _____ the advantages and disadvantages very carefully.
3   You can _____ us to give you our full support at the meeting.
4   Jane's very musical. She _____ her mother, who's a professional pianist.
5   David used to like French at school, but he _____ it when they started reading serious literature and not just funny stories.
6   Yes, I _____ you. Your explanation is very logical.

3 Intransitive + particle + preposition

> **come up against someone/something**
> **put up with someone/something**

Structure

A verb combines with a particle and a preposition. The pattern is intransitive, i.e. there is no direct object. The preposition introduces a noun phrase or pronoun (i.e. the object of the preposition). The words *someone* and *something* indicate the position and nature of the object of the preposition.

Study these examples and their meanings.

Verb	Particle	Preposition	Object of preposition	Meaning
come	up	against	someone/ something	be confronted with someone/ something
put	up	with	someone/ something	tolerate someone/ something

Stress

The particle is stressed:

come 'up against someone/something
put 'up with someone/something

Now study these phrasal verbs, their meanings and the examples, then use them in the exercises following.

come up against someone/something be confronted with or opposed by someone/something. *We didn't expect to come up against so many problems.*

come up with something produce or find a solution or idea. *Ann usually comes up with the right answers.*

get down to something tackle something; start serious work on a task, etc. *Learning English idioms isn't so difficult, once you get down to it.*

go in for something be very interested in a hobby or sport. *David goes in for collecting antique weapons. He has hundreds.* (EI 124)

look up to someone admire and respect someone. *Ray has always looked up to his uncle, who's a very successful actor.*

put up with someone/something tolerate or bear someone/something. *I've put up with her complaints long enough.*

Exercise 7

Complete the sentences with the correct particle or preposition.

▷ When the new houses were being built in our neighbourhood, we had to put ____ with a lot of noise.
up

1 The headmistress is very competent. All the teaching staff look ____ to her.
2 Liz goes in ____ modern art. She visits all the local exhibitions.
3 Did anyone come ____ with any good suggestions at the meeting?
4 The flight was delayed, so we had to put up ____ a long wait.
5 If you come ____ against any unexpected problems, let me know.
6 The examination is next week, so I must get ____ to some serious work.

Exercise 8

Replace the words in *italics* with a phrasal verb in its correct form.

▷ When George *is confronted with* tough competition he soon becomes discouraged.
comes up against

1 Why do you *tolerate* these continual interruptions? Tell everyone that you're busy and don't want to be disturbed!   ⟶

2 People *admire and respect* Richard because he's clever and successful. He has a very good reputation as a lawyer.

3 It's a difficult problem. I don't expect that we shall *produce* the answer at once.

4 Sally *is interested in* all kinds of water sports. Diving, water-skiing, sailing, you name it.

5 Diane's tennis is better than ever. So far this year she hasn't *been confronted with* anyone who can beat her.

6 It's time you *did some serious work on* learning your chemistry formulas. The test is next week.

Exercise 9

Complete the sentences with the most appropriate phrasal verb in its correct form.

▶ Jill's a bright child. She soon _____ the right answer.
comes up with/came up with

1 I refuse to _____ his bad behaviour any longer.

2 Our proposal _____ a lot of opposition at first, but in the end it was accepted.

3 Peter _____ sky-diving. He has some expensive equipment.

4 You'll have to produce better work if you want your colleagues to _____ you.

5 If you're short of good ideas, ask Liz. She usually _____ something imaginative.

6 Once you _____ learning English phrasal verbs, you will find them quite fascinating.

4 Transitive+particle

> **pack something in**
> **take someone off**

This combination represents the largest group of transitive patterns. It is perhaps the most difficult group to use because the direct object is not always in the same position.

Structure

A verb combines with an adverbial particle. There is always a direct object. The position of the direct object varies (see below).

Study these examples and their meanings.

Verb	Direct object	Particle	Meaning
pack	something	in	finish with or leave something
take	someone	off	imitate someone in a humorous way

Position of the direct object

The position of the direct object depends on whether it is a noun/noun phrase or a pronoun (*me*, *him*, *it*, *us*, etc.).

1 Noun/noun phrase as direct object
When the direct object is a noun or noun phrase, it can stand either *before* the particle or *after* the particle:

(a) *She packed her job in.*
(b) *She packed in her job.*

If the noun phrase is long (as a guide-line four words or more), choice (b) is preferable so that the particle is not placed too far away from the verb. Look at the length of the noun phrases and their positions in the following sentences:

>   *She packed a well-paid job in.*
> or *She packed in a well-paid job.*
> but *She packed in a job that was well-paid but stressful.*

>   *He took George Bush off.*
> or *He took off George Bush.*
> but *He took off George Bush and some other politicians.*

2 Pronoun as direct object

When the direct object is a pronoun (*me, you, him, her, it, us, them*), it must stand *before* the particle:

>   *She packed it in.*
>   *He took him off.*

Here are some more examples:

>   *I rang my brother up/I rang up my brother.*
> but *I rang him up.* (i.e. I telephoned him.)
>   *She brought six boys up/She brought up six boys.*
> but *She brought them up.* (i.e. She raised/reared them.)

There are some phrasal verbs of this pattern that do not follow the above rules but have a fixed direct object position. See page 23 at the end of this section for these exceptions.

Stress

When the phrasal verb is in isolation, e.g. for learning purposes, the stress is always on the particle. The stress is also on the particle when the direct object is a pronoun:

>   *She packed it 'in.*
>   *He took him 'off.*

Sentence stress applies in other cases:

>   *She has packed her 'job in and has gone to 'India.*
>   *He can take George 'Bush off 'beautifully.*

Now study these phrasal verbs, their meanings and the examples, then use them in the exercises following.

bring someone up raise or rear a child. *She brought six boys up.*

call something off cancel something. *We'll have to call the barbecue off. It's going to rain.*

let someone down disappoint someone. *I trusted Jeff, but he let me down badly.*

pack something in leave or end something (a job, a relationship, etc.) *She's packed her job in and has gone to India.*

ring someone up telephone someone. *He rang his brother up.*

take someone off imitate someone in a humorous way. *He can take George Bush off beautifully.*

Exercise 10

Complete the sentences with the correct particle.

▶ The headmistress called _____ the staff meeting, as several teachers were ill.
off

1 Brian didn't like his new job, so he packed it _____ after only three months.
2 Jimmy was taking _____ his maths teacher when unfortunately she walked in and caught him.
3 Where were you brought _____? In a town or in the country?
4 I'll ring you _____ this evening, after eight o'clock.
5 I'm relying on you to do good work, so please don't let me _____.
6 'Who won the cricket match?' 'No one. We had to call it _____ because it rained.'

Exercise 11

Complete the sentences with the correct verb in its correct form.

▶ I told the baby-sitter that you are good children, so don't _____ me down.
let

1 The tennis finals had to be _____ off because one of the players had hurt her ankle.
2 Paul _____ up just before lunch to say that he's coming to see us this evening.
3 I was born in Scotland and _____ up in Yorkshire.
4 That was very good! I didn't know that you could _____ off Mrs Thatcher.

───────────────→

5   David promised to help. I'm sure he won't _____ you down.
6   Mike's unhappy. He says he feels like _____ everything in and making a new start in another country.

Exercise 12

Replace the words in *italics* with a phrasal verb in its correct form.

▶   The meeting was *cancelled* at the last minute.
called off

1   Peter has stopped expecting people to help. He's been *disappointed* so many times in the past.
2   Why don't you *telephone* your parents and ask them if you can stay with us tonight?
3   Mrs Smith has had a hard life. She had to *raise* four children on very little money.
4   Are you quite sure that *ending* your relationship with Sarah is the right thing to do?
5   Tom is very good at *imitating* some famous pop stars.
6   *Cancel* all plans for this afternoon. We have to make an urgent trip to London.

Exercise 13

Ask questions with *who* or *when* and replace the words in *italics* with a pronoun (*him, her, it, them*).

▶   Sally called *the meeting* off at the last minute. (Who . . .?)
Who called it off?

Jim rang up *his brother*. (When . . .?)
When did Jim ring him up?

1   Steven let *Jeff* down again. (Who . . .?)
2   Jack packed *his job* in. (When . . .?)
3   An aunt brought *the children* up. (Who . . .?)
4   Mary Jones rang *Helen* up last night. (Who . . .?)
5   Mr Jackson called off *the staff meeting*. (When . . .?)
6   Barry Williams can take off *all the cabinet ministers*. (Who . . .?)

Exercise 14

Replace the pronouns (in *italics*) with the noun phrase in brackets ( ). Where there are two possibilities for the word order, give both.

▶ I rang *him* up. (the manager)

I rang the manager up.
I rang up the manager.

I rang *him* up. (the manager in charge of the complaints department)

I rang up the manager in charge of the complaints department.

1   Who brought *them* up? (the children)
2   Who brought *them* up? (the children who lost their parents in a car accident)
3   They called *it* off. (the cricket match)
4   They called *it* off. (the cricket match against the team from Perth)
5   She packed *it* in. (her boring job)
6   She packed *it* in. (a boring job without prospects)
7   We rang *them* up. (the Robinsons)
8   We rang *them* up. (the Robinsons who live in Brighton)
9   She took *her* off. (Margaret Thatcher)
10 She took *her* off. (Margaret Thatcher making a speech)

Pattern 4 exceptions

Direct object before the particle

Some phrasal verbs following this pattern have a direct object whose position is not flexible. Whether it is a noun phrase or a pronoun, the direct object must stand *before* the particle. This is necessary in order to differentiate phrasal verbs of this pattern, e.g. **get someone round**, from pattern 2 phrasal verbs, e.g. **get round someone**. The two verbs have quite different meanings:

I got Tom round to repair the lawn-mower.
= I asked Tom to my house to repair the lawn-mower.
I got round Tom to repair the lawn-mower.
= I managed to persuade Tom to repair the lawn-mower.

There are other pattern 4 phrasal verbs which also usually put the direct object *before* the particle, even when there is no similar pattern 2 phrasal verb. Here are some common ones which are used in this book:

get someone down depress someone. *This bad weather is getting everybody down.*

lead someone on mislead someone; try to persuade or encourage someone to believe something. *Clever salespeople are good at leading customers on so that they buy things that they don't need.*

see someone off accompany someone to his place of departure (station, etc.) *Are you going to the airport to see your friends off?*

tie someone down restrict someone's freedom/actions/ movement. *His broken leg really tied poor Tom down. He was in plaster for six weeks.*

Noun or noun phrase object after the particle

In contrast, there are a small number of pattern 4 phrasal verbs which usually have their noun or noun phrase object *after* the particle. However, as with all pattern 4 phrasal verbs, if the direct object is a pronoun it stands *before* the particle. Here are some common phrasal verbs of this type:

give up something stop doing something or indulging in something one likes or enjoys. *He had to give up beer and cigarettes.* But *He had to give them up.*

keep up something continue a friendship/an activity/a topic of study. *We've kept up our friendship for over twenty years.* But *We've kept it up.* (EI 128)

take up something begin to pursue a hobby/interest/sport, etc. *Patsy has taken up riding at the weekends.* But *She has taken it up.* (EI 149)

5 Transitive+preposition

> **talk someone into something**
> **turn someone off someone/something**

This combination represents a small group of transitive phrasal verb patterns. It is easy to use because the position of the direct object does not vary.

Structure

A verb combines with a preposition. The pattern is transitive, i.e. there is a direct object. The preposition introduces a noun phrase or pronoun object.

Study these examples and their meanings.

Verb	Direct object	Preposition	Object of preposition	Meaning
talk	someone	into	something	persuade someone to agree to something
turn	someone	off	someone/ something	cause someone to lose interest in someone/ something

Stress

When the phrasal verb is in isolation, e.g. for learning purposes, the stress is on the preposition. The stress is also on the preposition when the object of the preposition is a pronoun:

Who talked you 'into it?
You used to like strawberries. What turned you 'off them?

Sentence stress applies in other cases:

Who talked you into 'coming here?
What turned you off 'strawberries?

Now study these phrasal verbs, their meanings and the examples, then use them in the exercises following.

land someone with something burden someone with something he does not want. *The boss has landed me with the conference organization again.*

read something into something interpret something wrongly; understand more than was said or meant. *He didn't say that he wouldn't come. You're reading more into his remark than was intended.*

rush someone into something cause someone to make a hurried decision without considering the consequences. *The estate agent tried to rush us into buying an old house.*

talk someone into something persuade someone to agree to (do) something. *The salesman tried to talk me into buying a caravan.*

turn someone off someone/something cause someone to lose interest in someone/something or to lose his taste for something. *The advanced course in literature turned me off French.*

Exercise 15

Complete the sentences with the correct preposition.

▷   At first Ron didn't want to enter the photo competition, but I managed to talk him _____ it.
into

1   If the boss tries to land you _____ another report, just say you can't do it this week.

2   Think carefully before you accept the job offer. Don't let the firm rush you _____ a decision that you might regret later.

3   Mr Miller used to be your favourite teacher. What turned you _____ him so suddenly?

4   Please don't try to talk me _____ going to the concert. I can't afford the time.

5   The Minister didn't actually say that he would cut taxes. We mustn't read more _____ his speech than he stated.

Exercise 16

Complete the sentences with the correct verb in its correct form.

▶ Don't let anyone _____ you into buying a new car. There's nothing wrong with your present one.
talk

1 Our last holiday _____ us off camping for good. It rained every day and there was nowhere to dry our clothes.
2 I don't think Ruth is ready for marriage. Paul shouldn't _____ her into it so quickly.
3 Who _____ you with the washing-up, Uncle Tom? That's Dad's job!
4 My answer is no and I won't be _____ into changing my mind, whatever you say to try to persuade me.
5 Stop _____ things into Robert's remarks. He meant what he said – no more, no less.

Exercise 17

Replace the words in *italics* with a phrasal verb in its correct form.

▶ John has no intention of going on holiday with me, but I think I'll be able to *persuade him to agree to* it.
talk him into

1 What *caused you to lose interest in* politics? I thought you intended to make it your career.
2 Please don't *burden Polly with* any extra work. She already has more to do than she can manage.
3 I didn't really want to sell my stamp collection, but the dealer *hurried me into making a decision about* it, by offering me a good price. Now I regret it.
4 Don't *interpret more from* the letter than it says. It says that Uncle Joe's very ill, but it doesn't say that he won't recover.
5 At first I said I wouldn't lend Ann the money, but eventually she *persuaded me to agree to* it.

6 Transitive+particle +preposition

> put someone up to something
> take someone up on something

Structure

A verb combines with a particle and with a preposition. The pattern is transitive, i.e. there is a direct object. The preposition introduces a noun phrase or pronoun object.

Study these examples and their meanings.

Verb	Direct object	Particle	Preposition	Object of preposition	Meaning
put	someone	up	to	something	persuade someone to do something bad
take	someone	up	on	something	accept something from someone

Stress

When the phrasal verb is in isolation, e.g. for learning purposes, the stress is on the particle. The stress is also on the particle when the object of the preposition is a pronoun:

Who put Jim 'up to it?
Did he take you 'up on it?

Sentence stress applies in other cases:

Who put Jim up to telling 'lies?
Did he take you up on your invi'tation?

Now study these phrasal verbs, their meanings and the examples, then use them in the exercises following.

bring someone in on something inform someone about something; give someone a part in something (e.g. a plot, a plan, a scheme). *We should bring Julia in on the scheme.*

fix someone up with something supply someone with something he needs. *Can you fix me up with a part-time job in the supermarket?*

make something up to someone compensate someone for something. *I'm sorry that I disappointed you. I promise that I'll make it up to you somehow.*

put something down to something explain something; give the reason for something. *We put his rude manner down to ignorance of our British customs.*

put someone up to something encourage someone to do something bad or undesirable. *Who put Steven up to the idea of selling his bicycle without asking his parents first?*

take someone up on something accept something (an offer, suggestion) from someone. *Did he take you up on your invitation?*

Exercise 18

Complete the sentences with the correct particle or preposition.

▶ I can't accept your offer at present, but I'll be happy to take you _____ on it at a future date.

up

1 Terry spent hours of his free time helping me to repair my car. I must make it _____ to him somehow.

2 We ought to bring Sally in _____ the plan. If we don't she'll ask a lot of awkward questions.

3 It was the new assistant who made the mistake. Don't be angry. Put it _____ to his inexperience.

4 I know that taking the car without my permission wasn't your own idea. Who put you _____ to it?

5 If you want to try to repair the car yourself, I could fix you up _____ the necessary tools.

⟶

6   I said we should go to the Natural History Museum and Pat took me up _____ my suggestion straightaway. So we went.

Exercise 19

Complete the sentences with the correct verb in its correct form.

▶   Barry failed his driving test. He _____ it down to nervousness.
put

1   Don't _____ anyone else in on the plan. If too many people know, we won't be able to keep it secret.

2   I shall be in Birmingham for the weekend. Can you _____ me up with somewhere to stay?

3   Brian wouldn't steal money on his own initiative. Someone must have _____ him up to it.

4   Ken offered to buy me a drink, so I _____ him up on it and ordered a large brandy.

5   I'm sorry that I forgot your birthday. I'll _____ it up to you by taking you out to dinner tonight.

6   We _____ Jim's bad temper down to the pressure of work. He's extremely busy at the moment.

Exercise 20

Replace the words in *italics* with a phrasal verb in its correct form.

▶   I suggest we *inform Jill about* our proposal. She may be able to help us with it.
bring Jill in on

1   Ben was sorry about his mistake. He *explained it as* lack of concentration. He was very tired.

2   Peter knows that he shouldn't climb over Mr Smith's fence. He's never done so before. I wonder who *encouraged him to do it*.

3   'Ann said that she would lend me fifty pounds.' 'Well, did you *accept her offer?*'

4   The neighbours are going to paint their house. I told them that we could *supply them with* brushes and buckets.

5   Don't *inform Tommy about* our discussion. If you do, he'll waste our time with silly suggestions, as usual.

6   I'm sorry you had to do my work while I was away. I'd like to *compensate you for it* in some way.

7 Nominalized forms

> **a breakdown**
> **a hold-up**

Nominalized forms are nouns derived from phrasal verbs. Some phrasal verbs have a nominalized form that is in wide use, such as **a breakdown, a hold-up**. Many do not have a nominalized form.

Structure

Most nominalized forms are derived from verb+particle combinations, i.e. from pattern 1 and pattern 4 phrasal verbs. Some are derived from pattern 2 phrasal verbs. Most nominalized forms have the structure *verb+particle* or *verb+ preposition*:

Pattern 1	**break down**	**a breakdown**
	break in	**a break-in**
Pattern 4	**hold someone up**	**a hold-up**
	mix something up	**a mix-up**
Pattern 2	**run through something**	**a run-through**

A few nominalized forms have the structure *particle+verb*, e.g. **upkeep, outlay**.

Stress

The stress is on the first element, whether it is a verb or a particle/preposition:

'breakdown, 'hold-up, 'upkeep, 'outlay

Spelling

Many nominalized forms can be written with or without a hyphen (-). It is often a matter of established usage or of personal choice although a good dictionary will provide guidance. However, nominalized forms which place the particle/preposition first are not hyphenated, as in **upkeep, outlay.**

Plurals

Where a plural is possible (i.e. where the nominalized form is countable), it is formed in the usual way with the addition of *-s*:

breakdowns, break-ins, hold-ups

For more information on nominalized forms, see *Oxford Dictionary of Current Idiomatic English*, Volume 1.

Now study these nominalized forms, their meanings and the examples, then use them in the exercises following.

breakdown mechanical failure (engine of vehicle, etc.) *Jack's car had another breakdown on the way to work. He didn't arrive until eleven o'clock.* (EI 107)

break-in entry into a building by force (by thief, etc.) *There was a break-in at the video shop last night. A lot of equipment was stolen.*

check-up thorough examination (usually medical). *You should go to your dentist for regular check-ups.*

fall-off decrease (numbers), deterioration (quality). *No one liked the new lecturer, so there was a gradual fall-off in attendance at his lectures.*

hold-up delay, stoppage. *There's been an accident on the motorway, so there's a big hold-up.* (EI 127)

mix-up mistake, muddle, misunderstanding. *There must be a mix-up with the dates. Mr Jones is supposed to come tomorrow, not today.*

outlay expenditure, amount of money spent. *The outlay for the computer software was lower than we had expected.*

run-through quick examination, discussion or rehearsal. *Do you need to give your speech another run-through or do you already know it by heart?*

upkeep (cost of) keeping something in good condition or repair. *It may be wonderful to own a big, old house, but think of the upkeep!*

Exercise 21

Replace the words or phrases in *italics* with a nominalized form of a phrasal verb.

▶ Where are the finished copies of the contract? What's the reason for the *delay?*
hold-up

1   Could we have a *quick discussion* of the final travel arrangements? A few things have been changed.
2   When did you last see your doctor for a *medical examination?*
3   Please make sure that the names on the list are correct this time. We don't want any more *mistakes*.
4   There has been a *decrease* in the number of hotel bookings this year.
5   How big was your initial *expenditure* for the laboratory equipment?
6   You may have enough money to buy a house with a large garden, but can you afford the *cost of maintaining it?*

Exercise 22

Complete the sentences with the correct nominalized form of a phrasal verb.

▶ The ＿＿ in profits indicates that something is wrong with the company's advertising policy.
fall-off

1   Our dentist says that children should go for regular ＿＿ twice a year.
2   There was an awful ＿＿ with the seating arrangements at the conference. Everyone was sitting in the wrong place!
3   There's obviously a ＿＿ with my visa application. It should have arrived by now.
4   Simon had another ＿＿ – on the motorway, unfortunately. He shouldn't have bought that old car.
5   I've given the figures a quick ＿＿. I think they're correct.
6   There have been three ＿＿ into supermarkets this week, all in the same area.

PART II

1   This section contains 48 exercises and 8 test exercises at various intervals. Exercises 1–10 deal with one phrasal verb only. The number of verbs used then gradually increases, the last exercises dealing with up to 20 phrasal verbs.

2   The phrasal verbs used in each exercise are given in the reference section at the beginning of each one, together with an explanation of their meaning. These reference sections should be studied thoroughly before the exercises are attempted. Ideally, the phrasal verbs should first be memorized and then the reference section covered up. Common phrasal verbs recur several times throughout the exercises. This means that the longer reference sections in the later exercises contain several familiar as well as new phrasal verbs.

3   The page references to *English Idioms* (e.g. EI 132) given after some phrasal verbs indicate the page on which *additional* meanings of the verb can be found. Phrasal verbs with similar meanings are also indicated.

4   The number in brackets after each phrasal verb indicates its pattern number as described in Part I. (n) means that it is a nominalized form of a phrasal verb.

5   Several exercises have two parts, A and B. Part A is usually controlled, i.e. there is only one correct answer, or only one phrasal verb structure is possible in the answer. Part B practises the phrasal verbs in another way, usually providing guided practice but allowing the student to add his or her own ideas.

6   Several exercises end with the section **Talking point** which encourages free use of the phrasal verbs learnt, mostly in relation to the student's own situation. Here the student can relate personal experiences or give personal opinions. These sections provide an opportunity for using phrasal verbs in class or group discussion, but they can also be written or given as homework.

7   Unless otherwise stated, exercises can be done in written or oral form in class with a teacher or as self-study work. Several exercises are especially suitable for pair or group work.

8   Certain exercises use authentic texts. Words which may prove difficult are explained, but students should make sure that they understand *all* the vocabulary before the exercise is attempted.

9   The key gives answers or suggestions for answers.

10   A full index lists all of the phrasal verbs used in the exercises.

1   PUTTING THINGS OFF

Study the phrasal verb, its meaning and the example, then name five things that you *sometimes/often put off*, and five things that you *never put off*, as in the examples.

Sometimes we put something off until later, usually because it is difficult or unpleasant.

put something off (4) postpone or delay something. *Don't put off going to the dentist's if you have toothache.*

Here are some ideas:

going to the doctor's/dentist's	learning English vocabulary
writing letters	making an unpleasant
making an excuse/apology	telephone call
taking an important decision	paying bills
doing the housework/the	difficult work/reports/essays
gardening/the ironing	business meetings/discussions/
doing homework	dental appointments

▶ **I sometimes put off doing the housework.**

I often put off making dental appointments.

I never put business meetings off.

2   THINGS YOU COULDN'T DO WITHOUT

Study the phrasal verb, its meaning and the example, then name six things that you *couldn't do without*. Say why, as in the example.

do without something (2) manage without something one needs. *Fiona uses her computer every day. She says she couldn't do without it.* (EI 115)

Here are some suggestions:

bicycle	car	computer	typewriter
English dictionary	tent	video recorder
alarm clock	radio	briefcase

▶ **I couldn't do without my bicycle . . .**

. . . because I go to work/school on it every day.

. . . because it's my only means of transport.

. . . because I like to cycle in my free time.

3   PUTTING UP WITH THINGS

A
You have just come back from a holiday that was not enjoyable. Study the phrasal verb, its meaning and the example. Then complete the sentences with suitable words from the list, saying what you had to put up with.

put up with something/someone (3) tolerate or bear something/someone unpleasant or annoying: *I won't put up with these excuses any longer! I demand to see the manager!*

a 4-hour delay	long queues
loud music at night	cold showers
the smell of paint	slow service
noise and dirt	

▶ The airport was very crowded, so . . .

we had to put up with long queues.

1 The hotel was being redecorated, so . . .
2 There was a building site just across the road, so . . .
3 Our room was close to the hotel disco, so . . .
4 Sometimes there wasn't enough hot water, so . . .
5 Our waiter was new and inexperienced, so . . .
6 On the return flight, the plane couldn't take off because of bad weather, so . . .

B
People working in certain jobs have to put up with various unpleasant working conditions. Here are some jobs and some of their possible disadvantages. Say what the people who do these jobs usually have to put up with, as in the example.

shop assistants	noise and dirt
factory workers	working outside in bad weather
nurses	being away from home
airline pilots	low pay
workers on a building site	irregular working hours
taxi-drivers	working at weekends
bus-drivers	difficult customers
postmen/postwomen	shift work
waiters/waitresses	long working hours

▶ **Shop assistants usually have to put up with long working hours. Sometimes they have to put up with difficult customers as well.**

Talking point

What sort of things do people who live in big cities have to put up with? (Ideas: traffic problems, noise, air pollution.) Do you think it's right that they should have to put up with them? What could be done about them to make life in cities more pleasant?

4 WHAT COULD THEY DO WITH?

A

Study the phrasal verb, its meaning and the example, then say what the people or things in the pictures could do with, as in the example.

---

do with something (2) (used with **can/could**) want, need, benefit from something. *I'm hot and tired. I could do with a nice, cool drink.* (EI 115)

▶ He . . .
He could do with a new bicycle.

1 She . . .

2 The car . . .

3 He . . .

4 She . . .

5 His clothes . . .

6 He . . . ⟶

B

Now imagine that you could do with these things. Write short sentences saying why.

a new typewriter	a good night's sleep
a new English dictionary	a long holiday
a book on English idioms	a new car/bicycle

▶ **I could do with a new typewriter because mine . . .**

. . . is broken.

. . . is very old.

. . . can't be repaired.

. . . isn't modern enough.

5 LOOKING THINGS UP

If we need information we often have to look it up.

Study the phrasal verb, its meaning and the example.

look something up (4) search for information in a book (dictionary, timetable, atlas, etc.) or on a map, etc. *If you don't know what the word means, look it up!*

cookery book	train/flight timetable	map
encyclopaedia	telephone directory	atlas
hotel guide	dictionary	street map

Now say where you would look up the information in the questions. The words in the list will help you. You might think of more than one place to look up some of the information.

▶ Cambridge, England

I would look Cambridge up on a map of England/in an atlas.

the New York Penta Hotel

I would look up the New York Penta Hotel in a New York hotel guide.

1 Chicago
2 the location of Trafalgar Square
3 the arrival times of flights to London from Paris
4 the address of the London Tourist Board
5 the Grand Hotel, Brighton
6 the word 'idiom'

7   George Stephenson
8   a recipe for Yorkshire pudding
9   the location of Mount St. Helens
10 times of trains from Oxford to London

6   GETTING ON WITH PEOPLE

Study the phrasal verb, its meaning and the example.

get on (with someone) (1, 3) have a good relationship (with someone); like someone's company. *Dave and Len get on at work but not socially.* (EI 120)

Say how you get on with these groups of people. Where suitable, use *usually* and *quite well/very well/not . . . at all well* and *best*, as in the examples.

1   people of your own age
    younger people
    children
    older people
2   your parents
    your brother(s)/sister(s)
    your husband/wife/partner
    other relations
3   your neighbours
    your flat-/room-mate
    your landlord/landlady
4   people who are interested in sport
    people who are interested in art or music
    people who share your interests
5   people who are similar to you in character and temperament
    people who are very different from you

▶ **I usually get on quite well with older people.**

   I don't usually get on very well with younger people.

   I don't get on at all well with children.

   I get on best with people of my own age.

Talking point

Think of some well known fictional characters from television, films or books (e.g. JR Ewing in *Dallas*, Sherlock Holmes) and discuss what makes them easy or difficult to get on with.

7 CUTTING DOWN

To save money we sometimes try to cut down on things.

Study the phrasal verb, its meaning and the example.

cut down (on something) (1, 3) reduce consumption of something; use or eat less of something; spend less on something. *It's difficult to cut down on luxuries when you're used to having them.*

Now think of as many ways as possible of cutting down on these things, as in the example. The vocabulary in brackets will give you some ideas.

1 the cost of telephone calls (important, short, cheap-rate times)
2 gas/electricity bills (lights, heating, TV/radio, baths/showers, washing-machine/dish-washer)
3 personal spending (e.g. books, clothes, eating out, holidays, petrol, presents)

▶ the cost of telephone calls

You can cut down on the cost of telephone calls . . .

. . . by making calls only when they're important.

electricity bills

You can cut down on electricity bills . . .

. . . by turning off unnecessary lights.

personal spending

You can cut down on personal spending . . .

. . . by borrowing books from a library instead of buying them.

8 I'VE RUN OUT!

We often run out of something at a bad time.

Study the phrasal verb, its meaning and the example.

In your opinion, when is the worst time to run out of these things? Use your imagination! Answer as in the examples.

run out (of something) (1,3) have no more of something; use up all one has of something. *We've run out of milk. You'll have to drink your tea without.*

tea	milk	toothpaste	coffee	eggs
washing powder		writing paper	stamps	petrol
ideas	money			

▷ tea

The worst time to run out of tea is . . .

. . . in the early morning.

. . . at breakfast time before the shops open.

. . . when you have visitors who won't drink coffee!

milk

The worst time to run out of milk is . . .

. . . when you want to make the baby's bottle.

. . . when you're making tea or coffee for visitors.

. . . when the children want cereal for breakfast.

9   FINDING OUT

A lot of people have to find out things when they are doing their jobs.

Study the phrasal verb, its meaning and the example.

find out something (4) get information about something; learn something by asking/study/research or by chance; discover the answer to something. *The police know that Jim isn't telling the truth, so they're trying to find out what really happened.*

A
Now say what these people try to find out in their work, as in the example.

1   a spy
2   a private detective
3   a doctor
4   a newspaper reporter
5   a market researcher
6   a car mechanic
7   a vet (veterinary surgeon)
8   a TV repairman

▷ a historian

A historian tries to find out . . .

. . . historical facts.

. . . about the past.

. . . what happened long ago.

──────────▶

B

Say how you would find out these things. Answer as in the example.

▶ the meaning of a word

I would find out the meaning of a word . . .

. . . by asking my teacher.

1 the price of a watch in a shop window
2 when the last bus home goes
3 the exchange rate of the US dollar
4 whether someone is telling the truth
5 your neighbour's telephone number
6 how to make pizza
7 how to play chess
8 how much money you have in your bank account

10 GIVING IT UP

Study the phrasal verb, its meaning and the example.

give up something (4) stop (doing) something one enjoys; stop indulging in something. *If you gave up smoking, your health would improve a lot.*

Say which of these things you *could easily*, *couldn't* or *wouldn't like to* give up, as in the examples.

smoking/cigarettes	your favourite sport
eating sweet things	your daily work-out
eating meat	going to the cinema
going to parties	your hobby
watching television	beer/wine/alcohol

▶ **I could easily give up eating meat.**

I couldn't give up watching television.

I wouldn't like to give up playing tennis.

Talking point

Have you got a personal habit that you ought to or are trying to give up? (Examples: biting your nails, reading the newspaper at table, etc.) Ask your partner, other students in your group or your teacher the same question.

What reasons do people have for giving up certain pleasures, foods, luxuries or hobbies? What reasons do they have for not giving them up?

11   FLYING MADE EASY

Study these phrasal verbs
and their meanings, then
study the advertisement
carefully before turning
the page.

drop off (1)	fall asleep (EI 116). (Also **nod off**, EI 133)
get off (1)	leave a vehicle or means of transport (EI 120)
get on (1)	enter or mount a vehicle or means of transport (EI 120)
take off (1)	leave the ground (aircraft) (EI 147)
wake up (1)	stop sleeping; become awake/conscious after sleep (EI 152)

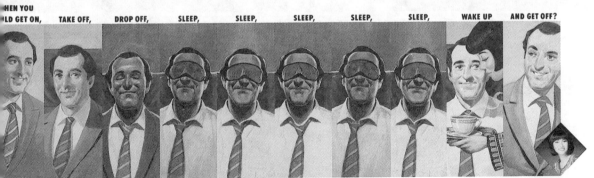

...y day of the week, a Singapore Airlines BIG TOP 747 flies non-stop from London to Singapore. No landing and take off en route, and so no interruption to your sleep. As with all aspects of our service this is, we assure you, quite unique.

SINGAPORE AIRLINES

Here is the same advertisement again, but this time the phrasal verbs are missing. Can you put them in? Two have been done for you.

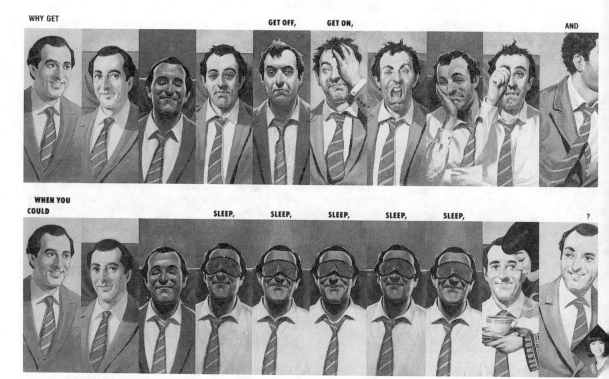

WHY GET

GET OFF, GET ON, AND

WHEN YOU COULD SLEEP, SLEEP, SLEEP, SLEEP, SLEEP, ?

Every day of the week, a Singapore Airlines BIG TOP 747 flies non-stop from London to Singapore. No landing and take off en route, and so no interruption to your sleep. As with all aspects of our service this is, we assure you, quite unique.

SINGAPORE AIRLINES

Talking point

Do you usually drop off in an aeroplane? Why do you think some passengers feel a little nervous when an aeroplane takes off? What should you do before you get off?

12   TALKING ABOUT YOURSELF

A
Study these phrasal verbs and their meanings, then use them in your answers to the questions. The suggestions in brackets will help you to answer.

bring someone up (4)	rear a child
go into something (2)	enter a career; take a job (EI 124)
grow up (1)	become adult; spend one's childhood years
settle down (1)	establish oneself; live permanently (EI 142)
take after someone (2)	resemble someone; have a similar character or appearance as a parent or member of one's family

1   Where did you grow up? (in a city/in the country/in this town)
2   Who brought you up? (my parents/my mother/an aunt)
3   Do you take after either parent or any other relative? If so, in what way? (in looks/temperament/character)
4   Where would you like to settle down? (in this country/abroad/in an English-speaking country/in a big city/in the country)
5   Are you likely to go into any of the following? If not, what do you think you are likely to go into?

teaching	nursing/medicine	journalism
business	politics	office/secretarial work

B
Ask your partner/other students in your English class the same questions.

Test exercise 1

(Exercises 1–12)

Complete the sentences with the appropriate phrasal verb in its correct form.

put something off
do without something
put up with something/someone
look something up
do with something
get on with someone
cut down on something
run out of something
find out something
give up something
drop off
get off
get on
take off
wake up
bring someone up
go into something
grow up
settle down
take after someone

1 Did you _____ what time the library opens?

2 The plane from Dallas _____ two hours late, so I missed my connecting flight from Frankfurt to London.

3 If you have anything important to do, do it straightaway. Don't _____ (it).

4 I'm afraid I've _____ sugar. We'll have to drink our coffee without.

5 Kathy says that she would like to _____ nursing. I think she would make a very good nurse.

6 I _____ in the country, but I've spent most of my life living in cities.

7 Jane plays the piano beautifully. She _____ her father who used to be a concert pianist.

8 Jeff is over forty and still a bachelor. I don't think he will ever _____.

9 I'm trying to lose weight by _____ bread and sweet things.

10 How do you _____ Mrs Brooks? Is she as unfriendly as people say?

11 I'm hot and tired. I could _____ a cold shower.

12 The bus is coming now. If you don't know where to _____, ask the bus driver. He'll tell you.

13 I can't _____ the hammering from the flat above much longer. It's giving me a headache.

14 Jim's parents were killed in an air crash when he was very young. An aunt _____ (him).

15 I missed the seven o'clock news on the radio this morning. I _____ too late.

16 I don't know what this word means, but I've got a Spanish dictionary here, so I'll _____ (it).

17 I watched a film on television last night, but I can't remember how it ended. I must have _____ before the end.

18 I use my pocket calculator every day. I couldn't _____ (it).

19 Here comes a bus. Before you _____, ask the driver if he stops near the library.

20 Tom used to be a professional football player, but he had to _____ (it) because of a knee injury.

13   PUZZLE: WHO'S GOING WHERE?

Here's a puzzle for you to solve.

First, study the phrasal verbs and their meanings.

brush up (on) something (4, 3)	revise one's past knowledge of something
check in (1)	register one's arrival
go off something (2)	lose one's liking for something
put up (1)	stay overnight
stop over (1)	break a long journey, usually for a night

Mike, Peter, Lucy, Diana and Bill are going on holiday.

One of them is going on a camping holiday by bicycle.

One of them is flying to Australia to visit an aunt.

One of them is going on a package holiday to Tenerife.

One of them is flying to Greece on a study trip.

One of them is touring Scotland by car, staying at different places.

Work out who's going where, using the information provided. Work alone, in pairs or in small groups.

Mike has gone off camping holidays.

One of the girls is brushing up her Spanish.

One of the girls is stopping over in Singapore.

Lucy doesn't speak a foreign language.

The boy touring Scotland will be putting up at guesthouses or bed and breakfast places.

Bill has to check in at the airport very early.

If you wish, use a grid to record the information, like this:

	Camping	Tenerife	Australia	Scotland	Greece
Mike	×				
Peter					
Lucy					
Diana					
Bill					

$\longrightarrow$

Talking point

1 What is the longest journey you have ever made by air? Did you stop over anywhere? If so, where did you put up?
2 Have you ever had to check in at an airport in the middle of the night? How did you feel about it? Did it make you go off flying?
3 Bed and breakfast places are very popular in Britain and in several other European countries. Have you ever put up at one? What was it like?
4 What advice would you give to someone wishing to brush up his/her English?
5 Apart from English, is there any other language that you would like to brush up on? Where would you go to brush it up?

14 SIMILAR PAIRS (1)

Study the phrasal verbs and their meanings very carefully. Then complete the dialogues in the pictures, adding a suitable pronoun in its correct position, as in the example.

get over something (2)	recover from a shock or unpleasant surprise, etc. (EI 121)
get something over (4)	complete something necessary and often unpleasant (EI 121)
get round someone (2)	persuade or coax someone. (Also **talk someone round**, EI 149)
get someone round (4)	call or summon someone to come to one's house, etc.
get through something (2)	complete something successfully (EI 122)
get something through (4)	cause something to be approved or accepted (EI 122)

▶ 'Harry wasn't chosen for the team. He's very disappointed.'
'Yes, I know, but he'll _____.'
get over it

1
'Dad refuses to let me go to
  the all-night pop concert.'
'Well, ask him again. Perhaps
  you can _____.'

2
'I've got work to do.'
'Yes, so I see. How long will it
  take you to _____?'

3
'I was sure we could repair the
  leak ourselves. I didn't want
  to ask the plumber and have
  to pay a huge bill.'
'Well, it's no good. We'll have
  to _____ now!'

4
'Now just relax. This isn't
  going to hurt.'
'Well, I'll certainly be glad to
  _____!'

5
'When do you need the visa?'
'Next week. How long will it
  take to _____?'

15 SIMILAR PAIRS (2)

Study the phrasal verbs and their meanings carefully.

pass on something (2)	not be able to give an answer to something (EI 134)
pass something on (4)	tell or give something to another person
see through someone (2)	recognize someone's deception; realize that someone is trying to deceive or mislead one
see someone through (4)	help someone through a difficult time
turn on someone (2)	attack someone physically or with words. (Also **set on someone**, EI 142)
turn someone on (4) (informal)	thrill/delight/excite someone

A
Write a short dialogue or paragraph showing a typical situation in which you would make these remarks/comments, as in the example.

▶ I'll have to pass on it.

'Next question. How big is Hyde Park?' 'Sorry, I have no idea. I'll have to pass on it.'

1 But I saw through him!
2 Then he turned on me.
3 All right. I'll pass it on.
4 I'll see you through.
5 It really turns me on!

B
Now work in pairs. One person reads out the first part of his/her dialogue or paragraph. The second person has to complete it with the correct remark/comment from the list.

16   IF I WERE PRIME MINISTER . . .

If you were the prime minister of your country, what laws would you make? What would you change?

Study the phrasal verbs
and their meanings.

bring something down (4)	reduce something (prices, spending)
bring something in (4)	introduce something
clamp down on something (3)	use one's authority to suppress something; take severe measures against something
put something up (4)	1 increase something 2 build or erect something (EI 138)
shut something down (4)	close something temporarily or permanently (factory, mine, business, etc.)
stamp something out (4)	get rid of something; suppress something totally

A
Use the phrasal verbs
together with the
suggested vocabulary here,
or think of ideas of your
own. Write down as many
sentences as you can
saying what you would do
if you were prime minister.
The examples will help
you.

laws against . . .	environmental pollution
taxation	old age pensions
crime	nuclear power stations
strict traffic laws	government spending
terrorists/terrorism	defence spending
kidnappers/kidnapping	drug-dealers/drug-dealing
racial violence	hospitals/schools/universities
hijackers/hijacking	food prices
unemployment	unprofitable industries
factories	private industry

▶ **If I were prime minister I would . . .**

. . . bring down taxation.

. . . put up old age pensions.

. . . try to stamp out crime.

→

B

Now play this game. You
need a good memory! One
person in the class or
group begins with a
sentence from his/her list.
The second person repeats
this sentence and adds to
it, and so on, like this:

Student 1:   **If I were prime minister I would bring down
taxation.**

Student 2:   **If I were prime minister I would bring down
taxation and put up old age pensions.**

Student 3:   **If I were prime minister I would bring down
taxation, put up old age pensions and try to
stamp out crime.**

If you make a mistake or miss something out, you drop out of
the game. The winner is the last student left.

17   PUZZLE: A ROUND-TABLE DISCUSSION

Study the phrasal verbs
and their meanings.

break in (1)   interrupt someone who is
                                          speaking (EI 107)

bring something up (4)   introduce something for
                                          discussion

come up with something (3)   produce an idea, suggestion,
                                          etc.

look on (1)   watch and/or listen inactively;
                                          not take part in an activity

nod off (1)   fall asleep (in a chair, etc.).
                                          (Also **drop off**, EI 116)

talk someone down (4)   silence someone by talking
                                          more oneself

Six men are sitting at a
table having a discussion.
Their names are *Smith*,
Jones, *Brown*, *Hill*, *Evans*
and *Walker*. The diagram
shows where Smith is
sitting.

Smith

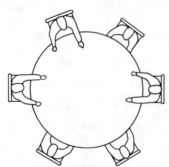

From this information, work out who's who and who's sitting where.

Smith keeps nodding off.

Brown is sitting next to Jones, who keeps breaking in.

Directly opposite Smith is someone who keeps bringing up unimportant matters.

The man who keeps breaking in is sitting next to Smith.

Hill is sitting on the right of Evans, who comes up with some good ideas.

The man with the good ideas is to the right of the man nodding off.

Jones is sitting to the right of a man who likes talking others down.

The man just looking on is next to the man with the good ideas.

If you have solved the puzzle correctly, you will be able to answer these questions:

1 Who is sitting between Hill and Brown?
2 Who likes to talk the others down?
3 Who just looks on?
4 What does Walker keep doing?
5 Who is sitting opposite the man who keeps breaking in?

Talking point

1 Do you like taking part in discussions? Why?
2 What do you think of people who keep breaking in when others are speaking?
3 Have you ever nodded off during a lecture or discussion? If so, why?
4 Do you often come up with good ideas or suggestions during discussions?
5 During discussions, do you usually take an active part or do you prefer to look on and listen?
6 Do you think it is impolite to talk others down?

Test exercise 2

(Exercises 13–17)

Complete the sentences with the appropriate phrasal verb in its correct form.

1 Have you ever _____ at a really luxurious hotel?

2 At first Jane refused to lend me her car, but I managed to _____ (her).

3 I'll phone you from the hotel as soon as I've _____.

4 We ought to discuss the matter as soon as possible. I'll _____ (it) at the meeting tomorrow.

brush up on something
check in

5 Come and help me to carry the boxes! Don't just stand there _____!

go off something
put up

6 Be quiet, David. You really shouldn't _____ when someone's speaking. It's impolite.

stop over
get over something

7 I've got a message for Peter from Linda. Could you _____ (it) when you see him this afternoon?

get something over
get round someone

8 Why did you suddenly stop eating meat? What made you _____ (it)?

get through something
pass something on

9 If you could go to an English-speaking country to _____ your English, which country would you choose?

see through someone
turn on someone

10 Sally is disappointed that she didn't get the job at the research laboratory, but she'll _____ (it).

bring something in
put something up

11 Marjory lied to me. She thinks that I don't know what she's planning. But I do. I can _____ (her).

shut something down
break in

12 Why did they _____ the factory in King Street? There are hundreds of people out of work now.

bring something up
come up with something

13 Governments should _____ international laws against terrorism.

look on
nod off

14 When we fly to Texas, we're going to _____ in Atlanta to visit some friends.

15 I wish the examination was tomorrow! I'm nervous, so I shall be glad to _____ (it).

16 Grandfather must be tired. He's _____ in his chair.

17 I've got a lot of work to do. I hope I can _____ (it) before the weekend.

18 I knew that Mr Brown would be annoyed when I told him about my mistake, but I didn't expect him to _____ (me) like that!

19 We haven't got much time. We'll have to _____ a solution to the problem soon.

20 They're _____ some new shops in North Street.

18   HELPING PEOPLE

How would/could you help in the following situations?

Study these phrasal verbs and their meanings. Then make sentences using a suitable phrasal verb and a pronoun (*him*, *her*, *it* or *them*) in its correct position.

break something up (4)   Stop a fight, quarrel, etc. (often by force)

bring someone round (4)   restore someone to consciousness (EI 109)

call on someone (2)   visit someone (EI 110)

drop something off (4)   deliver or take something somewhere/to someone

go over something (2) **(with someone)**   repeat an explanation of something (EI 124)

pick someone up (4)   collect or go to get someone (often in a vehicle) (EI 135)

put someone up (4)   give accommodation to someone (EI 138)

▶ A former friend contacts you. He/She is visiting your town and needs somewhere to stay for two nights.
What would you offer to do?

I would offer to put him/her up at my house/flat.

1   A member of your English class needs help with an exercise. You have already done it.
How could you help?

2   A girl faints. You are the only other person close by.
What would you try to do?

3   Some friends are arriving back from holiday. They have a lot of luggage but no transport from the airport. You have a car.
What would you offer to do?

4   An elderly person living alone in your neighbourhood would be glad to have someone to talk to.
What could you try to do?

5   A friend would like to borrow some of your records and cassettes. You will be passing his/her house on the way to the library.
What could you do?

6   You see two boys fighting. The smaller boy is losing the fight.
What would you try to do?

⟶

Talking point

1 Have you ever had to break up a fight?
2 Have you ever tried to bring someone round?
3 How often do you call on your friends? How often do your friends call on you?
4 Have you got a car? If so, do you often pick people up in it? When was the last time that someone picked you up?
5 When was the last time that you/your parents put someone up? Do you/your parents often put people up? Has a friend ever put you up?

19 WHAT NEEDS DOING?

Study these phrasal verbs and their meanings.

clean something up (4)	remove dirt from something
clear something out (4)	empty something of unwanted things (room, drawer, etc.)
do something up (4)	renovate something (EI 115)
finish something off (4)	complete something
sort something out (4)	put something in order or into a system
tidy something up (4)	make something tidy or neat in appearance
touch something up (4)	improve the appearance of something by making small changes, e.g. renewing paint

A

Now say what needs doing in the pictures, as in the example.

▶ The papers . . .

The papers need sorting out.

1 The old house . . .

2 The garden shed . . .

3 The study . . .

4 The paintwork . . .

5 The new fence . . .

6 The old silver
   candlestick . . .

B

What needs doing in your room/house/flat? Try to think of at least six things. These words will give you some ideas.

my bedroom	my car	my old books	our house
my writing-desk	my bicycle	my old newspapers	our kitchen
my cupboards	my homework	my photographs	our garage
my drawers	my essay	my letters	our attic

20 WHAT HAPPENED?

Imagine that you witnessed a traffic accident and have been asked to describe what happened. Write a report on what you saw, using all or any of the phrasal verbs given. The suggested vocabulary will give you some ideas.

cut in (1)	drive sharply in front of another vehicle after overtaking (EI 113)
drive off (1)	drive away; leave
hold something up (4)	delay or stop something (EI 127)
pull out (4)	move out of a line of traffic or a parking space
run into something (2)	drive into something and cause an accident
speed up (4)	increase speed
turn off (4)	drive right or left at a junction or crossroads

sportscar	delivery van	impatient	overtake
junction	traffic lights	brake suddenly	

Talking point

1 Have you ever run into anything with your car or bicycle? If you have, describe to the class what happened.
2 What do you think of drivers who cut in?
3 What kind of vehicles often hold the traffic up?
4 As a driver/cyclist, what should you do before you turn off? What could happen if you don't?

21 THE LAW AND YOU

Here is a letter written to *The law and you*, the legal advice column of a popular British magazine.

Study these phrasal verbs and their meanings.

come out (1)	become public; be made known (EI 112)
come to something (2)	be a matter or question of something (EI 113)
end up (1)	finally be somewhere or do something; finish (as)

make off (1)	hurry away to avoid punishment
pay up (1)	pay all the money one owes
run off (1)	run away
slip out (1)	leave quickly and quietly so as not to be noticed

Now read the letter and the reply, putting in the missing phrasal verbs in their correct form, as in the example.

*I have done something very silly and I don't know what to do. The other day, I had lunch in a café I often use, but when it **came to** paying the bill, I discovered that I had forgotten my purse. I was too embarrassed to say anything, so I just __1__ without paying. Now I haven't got the nerve[1] to go back, in case I'm arrested. I'm terrified that it will all __2__ and I will __3__ in court and lose my job.'*

You were very silly to __4__ like that. Whyever didn't you just explain you would pay later? They might have asked you for some identification and your name and address, but that's all. Now you have laid yourself open[2] to the charge of 'making off without payment' contrary[3] to section three of the Theft Act 1968. This is committed where a person __5__ without paying, intending never to pay.

You would do well to go back to the café, explain what happened, apologize and __6__. If you feel that you can't do that, at least send the money by post with a covering[4] letter.

[1]courage
[2]exposed yourself
[3]against
[4]accompanying

Talking point

Have you ever been in a similar situation? If so, did you make off like the woman in the article or did you explain and try to work out a solution? Tell your experience to the class. If not, imagine what you would have done.

22 MORNING ROUTINE

Study these phrasal verbs and their meanings, then use a suitable phrasal verb to describe what Paul and Jeff usually do in the mornings.

get up (1)	get out of bed (EI 122)
get someone up (4)	call someone from bed (EI 122)
lie in (1)	stay in bed longer than usual
pick someone up (4)	collect or go to get someone (EI 135)
set off (1)	leave home, begin a journey
stop off (1)	break a journey for a short time
wake up (1)	stop sleeping, become awake/conscious after sleep (EI 152)

▶ Paul . . .

Paul gets up at seven o'clock.

1 He . . .

2 He usually . . .

3 On Sundays . . .

4 Jeff . . .

5 His mother . . .

6 He . . .

7 On the way to school he . . .

Talking point

1 What time do you usually wake up on weekdays?
2 Do you usually get up immediately?
3 Does anyone have to get you up?
4 What time do you usually set off for work/school?
5 Do you stop off anywhere on your way to work/school?
6 Do you lie in on Saturdays and Sundays?

Now ask other students in your class these questions. Ask your teacher as well!

Test exercise 3

(Exercises 18–22)

Complete the sentences with the appropriate phrasal verb in its correct form.

bring someone round
call on someone
drop something off
go over something
pick someone up
put someone up
clear something out
sort something out
finish something off
cut in
hold someone/
  something up
pull out
speed up
turn off
end up
make off
slip out
get up
lie in
set off

1 'Where did the blue van go?' 'It _____ to the right at the traffic lights.'
2 The old lady fainted, but the nurse was soon able to _____ (her).
3 'What are all these old books and photographs doing on the floor?' 'They were all in the attic – we've been _____ (it)'.
4 Why don't you _____ Aunt Mary when you're in Liverpool? She would be delighted to see you.
5 We almost had an accident on the motorway. A motor-cyclist _____ in front of us, so I had to brake suddenly.
6 I don't need to book a hotel room in Manchester. Joan has offered to _____ (me).
7 I really must _____ these old newspapers. I want to keep some and throw away the rest.
8 I'm glad you're coming to the party with me. I'll _____ (you) at seven o'clock. Be ready!
9 I don't understand how to do this mathematics homework. Would you _____ (it) with me, please?
10 I've still got some books of yours. If you're at home this evening, I'll _____ (them) on my way from the office.
11 I'm sorry I'm late. I was just leaving home when the telephone rang, so the call _____ (me).
12 I go to bed late, so I don't usually _____ before eight o'clock.
13 If Jim doesn't drive his sportscar more carefully, he'll _____ in hospital.
14 I had to leave the meeting half way through. I managed to _____ without disturbing anyone.
15 If you want to be in London by lunch-time, you'll have to _____ from here very early.
16 It's Sunday tomorrow. I shall _____ until ten o'clock!
17 I'll help you with the washing-up as soon as I've _____ this letter.
18 When the van driver realized that the police were following him, he started to _____.
19 The little boy took an apple from the farmer's tree, then he _____ as fast as he could.
20 There's no traffic coming at the moment, so it's safe to _____.

23 DOING PUZZLES (1)

Most people enjoy the challenge of solving a puzzle. Here the authors of a book on puzzles give some hints on how to solve them.

First, study these phrasal verbs and their meanings.

catch someone out (4)	trick or outwit someone
come across something (2)	meet or encounter something; find something by chance
give up (1)	lose interest and admit defeat
look out for something (3)	be alert so as to see something
move on (to something) (1)	go further/forward; proceed to the next task, etc.
read through something (2)	read something from beginning to end
think about something (2)	consider something (EI 149)
work something out (4)	calculate something, find the answer to something by careful thinking

Now complete these hints on solving puzzles with the most appropriate phrasal verb. Use one phrasal verb twice.

When you are doing puzzles, always __1__ the question carefully, bit by bit. __2__ what each part means as you read. If you can't __3__ the answer after a little thought, you may be on the wrong track. Try going back to the beginning again and thinking in a different direction. Don't __4__ too quickly – the answers are often quite obvious once you begin to look at the puzzle in the right way. Don't forget to __5__ trick questions either. Some puzzles are deliberately designed to __6__ (you) and often sound much more difficult than they really are. Take your time, too – it doesn't matter how long it takes you to __7__ the answers. You will find some puzzles easier than others. If you __8__ one that seems too difficult, leave it and __9__ to another. It may seem easier when you come back to it another time.

Now try the puzzles in the next exercise!

24 DOING PUZZLES (2)

Many puzzles use phrasal verbs, asking the reader to work things out, sort things out or fill things in, for example. Some of the instructions are missing from these puzzles.

Study these phrasal verbs and their meanings, then complete the instructions using the most appropriate phrasal verb. If you think two phrasal verbs are possible in some cases, write both.

Can you do the puzzles?

fill something in (4)	complete something (by writing in the information required)
find out (1)	discover; get information about something
fit in with someone/ something (3)	match or be similar to someone/ something
fit something in (4)	find space for something; put something into the appropriate space
mix something up (4)	confuse or muddle something; put something in the wrong order
sort something out (4)	put something in the correct order
work something out (4)	calculate something; find the answer to something by careful thinking

▷ Can you _____ the spaces with the four-letter words to make six-letter words?

fill in

O----E P----T T----Y   LANE WENT RANG

1 It takes two people two days to dig two holes. _____ how long it takes one person to dig one hole.

2 The book titles are _____ . _____ the letters to _____ what the titles are. The authors' names will help you.

RUREMD SI SYAE   HET HTRIYT-EINN TSPES
Agatha Christie   John Buchan

HET LOD NMA DNA TEH AES
Ernest Hemingway

3 A, B, C and D want to hold a tennis tournament. They all have to play against each other once. Can you _____ how many matches will be played?

4   Which figure does not _____ the others?

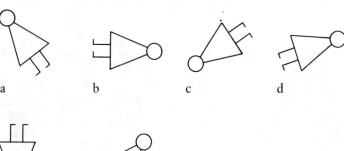

a   b   c   d

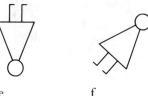

e   f

5   Complete the series by _____ the missing numbers.

a) 4   5   7   11   19   ?
b) 64   48   ?   36   34   33

6   The letters of five countries are _____. Can you _____ (them)?
     Which country does not _____ the others?

   RCEGEE   TAYIL   GADENNL
   RFANEC   IDANI

7   Can you _____ which three-letter words end one word and
     start another?

   RAB(---)TER   CAR(---)ROL   HAP(---)CIL

8   Complete the series by _____ the missing letters.

a) A   C   E   G   I   ?
b) A   A   E   B   I   ?   O   D   U   E

9   The numbers **2, 4, 6** and **8** are missing from the number puzzle.
     Where do they go? Can you _____ (them)?

```
          9       =   15
    3     5   7   =   15
          1       =   15
    =     =   =
    15   15  15
```

10   Time puzzle. These pictures show people who lived long ago, but the chronological order is wrong. Can you _____ (them)? Put them in the order in which they lived.

1   2   3

4   5

Now check your answers with the key.

25   CHECK YOUR HEALTH HABITS!

How would you try to improve your health and eating habits?

Study these phrasal verbs and their meanings, then make as many sentences as you can, using the suggested words (or others!) as in the examples.

cut down on something (3)	reduce consumption of something
cut something out (4)	exclude something (EI 114)
do without something (2)	manage without something one wants or usually has (EI 115)
give up something (4)	stop (doing/having) something one enjoys
stick to something (2)	adhere to or persevere with something

take up something (4)	begin doing something regularly (sport, hobby, interest)
work something off (4)	lose or get rid of something (weight, energy)
work out (1)	do physical fitness exercises

sweet things	fat and sugar	smoking
a diet	strong coffee	alcohol
health foods	carbohydrates	sport
surplus weight	fitness training	salads
meat	fish and vegetables	chocolate
salt	fried foods	Coca-Cola

▶ **I would take up sport.**

I would cut out sweet things.

I would stick to a diet.

26 CARTOON HUMOUR

Here are some cartoons from *Punch*, a weekly magazine well known for its humour and satire. They all use a phrasal verb.

Study these phrasal verbs and their meanings, then match the cartoons on the next page with the appropriate text.

come across (1)	be understood clearly
end up (1)	finally be somewhere or do something; finish (as)
keep up something (4)	continue with something; do something regularly
make something up (4)	invent something (story, joke, excuse) (EI 132)
pass something on (4)	tell another person something
pick something up (4)	go to get something (EI 135)
put up something (4)	lend or contribute something (money, etc.) (EI 138)
turn something off (4)	stop or disconnect something (electricity, etc.)

——————————————→

1

2

3

4

5

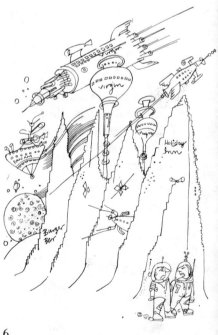

6

A 'Somebody's Daddy obviously didn't keep up the maintena
 payments.'
B 'The rest of our luggage either ended up in a black hole[2] o
 been sent to planet Zong.'
C 'Nine light years[3] from home, and now you remember that you
 forgot to turn off the gas.'
D 'OK, everyone's gone – you can pick it up now.'
E 'Letting him come was the only way I could get him to put up the
 money to pay for all this.'
F 'On our left is Traitor's Gate[4]. Pass it on.'

[1] Maintenance payments are payments made by a man to support his
former wife and children when they divorce.
[2] A black hole is an area in space into which things disappear.
[3] A light year is used as a measurement of time in space.
[4] Traitor's Gate, at the Tower of London, is a popular tourist
attraction. Prisoners passed through this gate on their way to
execution.

Talking point

1 In your opinion, which cartoon comes across best? Why?
2 Which cartoon do you like best? Why?
3 Do you think making up cartoons and jokes is easy or difficult?
4 Are you good at making up or telling jokes? What do you find
 difficult about telling jokes?

27 PEOPLE AND THEIR JOBS

People doing certain jobs usually show a special ability or liking
for what they do.

Study the phrasal verbs
and their meanings.

deal with someone (2)	be concerned with someone; have contact with someone (EI 114)
draw someone out (4)	encourage someone to speak about himself or his problems
dress up (1)	put on clothes for a special occasion
find out something (4)	get information by inquiry or study; discover facts, etc.
get about (1)	travel to different places (EI 119)

look after someone (2)	take care of or be responsible for the well-being of someone
make something up (4)	invent something (a joke, an excuse, a story) (EI 132)
put something across (4)	express or communicate something (an explanation, information)
talk someone into something (5)	persuade someone to agree to something. (Also **talk someone round**, EI 149)

Now make sentences, saying what people who do these jobs are *usually good at* doing and/or *usually like* doing, as in the examples. The suggested vocabulary will give you some ideas.

private investigator	people
nurse	things
teacher	children
door-to-door salesman	animals
psychoanalyst	explanations
travel courier	ideas
zoo-keeper	information
novelist	stories
journalist	
police detective	
fashion model	

▶ **A private investigator is usually good at finding out information about people.**

A nurse . . .

. . . is usually good at dealing with people.
. . . usually likes looking after people.

Talking point

Use the phrasal verbs and the words given in the list (or your own words!) to say what you are good/not good at doing, and what you like/don't like doing.

28   RENTING A CAR IN THE UK

Study the phrasal verbs
and nominalized forms
and their meanings.

back-up (n)	additional service (EI 104)
breakdown (n)	technical defect causing a vehicle to stop functioning (EI 107)
drive off (1)	drive away; leave in a car/vehicle
drop something off (4)	take something somewhere and leave it there
end up (1)	finally be somewhere or do something; finish (as)
get out (1)	go out and enjoy oneself (EI 121)
go about something (2)	manage/approach/tackle something
pick something up (4)	go to get or collect something (EI 135)
take someone out (4)	invite and accompany someone to a place of entertainment (EI 148)

Here is a letter to a
column called *We can help*
which appears in a weekly
magazine, with the reply.
Read the text and put in
the missing phrasal verbs
in the correct form, as in
the example.

Make the most of the summer by **getting out** on the road.

During the school holidays my wife and I would like to __1__ the children for a few days. The trouble is that we don't have a car, so how do we __2__ hiring one for the weekend?

Look first in your local *Yellow Pages*[1]. There you'll find a list of national car hire firms. Or, if you prefer, smaller firms often advertise in the local press. They'll sometimes offer cheaper deals but not the __3__, such as a __4__ service, that's provided by the bigger agencies. For a weekend's hire, expect to pay between £32 and £50 for a small car, like a Metro. Larger cars will cost more. When you go along to __5__ your car, it's a good idea to inspect it to see there are no scratches or faults for which you might later be blamed.

The bigger firms will automatically insure you for collision[2] damage, but some smaller companies may include only third party insurance[3] in their charge. So make sure you're covered[4], or you could __6__ with a big bill if the car is damaged in any way. Usually you will be given a tank of petrol before you __7__, which you're expected to replace when you bring the car back. If you have hired the car for the weekend, most firms will ask you to __8__ (it) at the original pick-up point.

[1] directory of businesses (printed on yellow paper)
[2] accident
[3] insurance for damage to another car
[4] fully insured

Test exercise 4

(Exercises 23–28)

Complete the sentences with the appropriate phrasal verb in its correct form.

catch someone out
come across something
look out for something
work something out
fill something in
mix something up
cut something out
stick to something
take up something
work something off
work out
keep up something
make something up
turn something off
deal with something
get about
look after someone
put something across
talk someone into
    something
go about something

1   If you want to lose weight, _____ potatoes, bread and sweet things for a week.

2   The oral examination was difficult. The examiner tried to _____ (me) by asking some tricky questions.

3   My brother has _____ karate. He trains three times a week.

4   Here are the visa application forms. You have to _____ (them) and return them to the consulate.

5   Grandmother's over eighty, but she still likes to _____. She's going to Paris next week.

6   I've joined a health and fitness club. I go there every day to _____ for an hour.

7   I don't believe the story Bob told us. I'm sure he _____ (it).

8   Who's going to _____ the dog next week when we go to Glasgow?

9   If you don't want to lend Jeff money, just say 'no'. Don't let him _____ (you) (it).

10 We don't know who's staying where. The secretary has _____ the hotel bookings.

11 If you see this sign in a shop window, you can pay by credit card. So remember, just _____ the sign.

12 The iron – I've forgotten to _____ (it). I must go back home at once.

13 If you've made a decision, _____ (it). Don't change your mind again.

14 If you jog every day, you'll soon _____ your surplus kilos.

15 Do you know what this word means? I haven't _____ (it) in our English books before.

16 'Have you got the answer to number seven in the maths exercise?' 'No. I haven't _____ (it) yet.'

17 I haven't seen Michael for over twenty years, but we have _____ our friendship by letter.

18 We would like to buy a holiday flat in Spain, but we don't know how to _____ (it).

19 George has some very good ideas, but he sometimes has difficulty in _____ (them) to others.

20 I'm sorry about the mix-up with your order, Sir. I'll _____ (it) at once.

29   RINGING PEOPLE UP

Several phrasal verbs are used in connection with telephoning.

Study these phrasal verbs and their meanings.

call/phone/ring (someone) back (1,4)	telephone (someone) again later
call/phone/ring (someone) up (1,4)	telephone (someone)
cut someone off (4)	break someone's telephone connection. (Often passive: **be cut off**, lose a telephone connection)
get back to someone (3)	contact someone later
get through (1)	get a telephone connection (EI 121)
hang up (1)	end a telephone call (often abruptly). (Also **ring off**, EI 139)
hold on (1)	wait
put someone through (4)	connect someone on the telephone

A

Make short dialogues for the given situations, using suitable phrasal verbs as in the example.

▶ A asks to be connected with Mr Johnson on extension 235. B tries to make the connection but Mr Johnson's number is engaged. B asks A if he would like to phone again later.

A: Good morning, could you **put me through** to Mr Johnson, please, on extension 235?

B: Just a moment, please, I'm trying to **put you through** . . . I'm sorry, but Mr Johnson's number is engaged. Would you like to **ring back** later?

1   Ann tells Bill that she has tried to phone him three times, but couldn't get a connection. Ann wants some information from Bill. Bill promises to contact Ann with the information later.

2   Mr Fox asks to be connected with the bank manager. A bank clerk tells Mr Fox that the bank manager will be free in a moment and asks him to wait.

3   Janet and Peter are speaking. Peter has to end the call as the door-bell rings. Janet asks Peter to phone again later.

$\longrightarrow$

4   Mark and Kate were speaking when the connection was suddenly lost. Now Mark rings Kate again and explains what happened. Kate says she thought Mark had ended the conversation abruptly for some reason.

5   Andy asks Terry to give him Robert's address. Terry asks Andy to wait until he gets his address book. Terry can't find it, so he tells Andy that he will contact him again later. Terry says he has to end the conversation now anyway. He's going out.

B
Now work with a partner and invent a short telephone dialogue using **get through, hang up, hold on** and **ring someone back**.

Talking point

1   On average, how many times a week do you ring up friends or members of your family? Who do you ring up most often?
2   How often do you ring up someone abroad?
3   When you make a call abroad, do you sometimes have difficulty getting through?
4   Have you ever been cut off during a conversation? What did you do?

30 HIT PARADE

The titles of pop songs often include phrasal verbs.

Study these phrasal verbs and their meanings, then complete the Top Ten song titles with the phrasal verbs given in brackets. Put the pronouns in their correct positions!

count on someone (2)	rely on someone
do without someone (2)	manage without someone
get over someone (2)	stop being emotionally involved with someone
get to someone (2) (informal)	influence someone's emotions or state of mind (EI 122)
lead someone on (4)	try to persuade or encourage someone to believe something which is untrue
let someone down (4)	disappoint someone
see someone through (4)	help someone through a difficult time/situation
stand by someone (2)	support and comfort someone
think something over (4)	consider something carefully

walk out on someone (3)   abandon/leave someone; end a relationship

work something out (4)   find a solution to a problem (EI 153)

▶   I'm still _____ (get over, you)
I'm still getting over you.

1   Don't _____ (let down, me)
2   We'll _____ (work out, it)
3   I'll _____ (see through, you)
4   If you _____ (stand by, me)
5   Let's _____ (think over, it)
6   You can always _____ (count on, me)
7   Since you _____ (walk out on, me)
8   But you were only _____ (lead on, me)
9   I just can't _____ (do without, her)
10   You're _____ (get to, me)

31   A PROBLEM SHARED

Study these phrasal verbs and their meanings.

bring something up (4)   mention or introduce something for discussion

get someone down (4)   depress someone

get on (with someone) (1, 3)   have a good relationship (with someone) (EI 120)

go about something (2)   approach or tackle a problem

have something out (with someone) (4, 6) (informal)   argue something to the end; discuss something thoroughly

look up to someone (3)   respect someone; have a very good opinion of someone

put in for something (3)   request or apply for something

put up with something (3)   tolerate something

see into something (2)   investigate or examine something. (Also **look into something**, EI 131)

talk someone into something (5)   persuade someone to agree to something

turn something down (4)   reject or refuse something

⟶

People often write to magazines about their problems. Read this letter and answer the questions.

Dear Emma

I have been a secretary in a small firm for five years. I enjoy the work and my employer has no reason for complaint. The trouble is that I don't earn enough money. My employer has never given me a salary increase, although I have put in for one every year. He hasn't exactly turned down my requests. He simply ignores them. Every time I bring the matter up, he always has some excuse or says that he will see into it. But he never does.

I would like to have it out with him, but I'm not sure how to go about it. I once threatened to leave, but he talked me into staying. Would it be better to leave after all? I want to stay. All the other workers look up to me and I get on with them, but the boss simply doesn't take me seriously.

The situation is getting me down and I feel I can't put up with it for much longer. Please advise me.

Margaret M.
Surrey

---

1   There are 11 phrasal verbs in the letter. Did you spot them all? Write them down in the order they appear.
2   What do they mean? Replace each phrasal verb with a word or phrase with the same meaning, as in the example.

▶   *put in for*
   applied for/requested

Talking point

What do you think Margaret M. should do? Should she put in for another rise? What shouldn't she do? What should or shouldn't her boss do?

32 TELEPHONE MESSAGES

A lot of telephone messages were recorded on your answering machine.

Study the phrasal verbs and their meanings.

ask someone out (4)	invite someone to go out for a meal, to the theatre, etc.
call for someone (2)	collect someone from his/her home, hotel, etc. (EI 110)
call something off (4)	cancel something
count on someone (2)	rely on someone
do without something (2)	manage without something one wants or usually has
keep someone up (4)	prevent someone from going to bed
pick someone up (4)	go to get someone (often in a vehicle) (EI 135)
put someone up (4)	give someone accommodation overnight (EI 138)
see someone off (4)	accompany someone to his place of departure (EI 141)
take someone on (4)	employ someone (EI 148)
take someone up on something (6)	accept someone's offer (EI 149)

A

First, complete the messages with the missing phrasal verbs in the correct form and put the pronouns in the correct position, as in the example.

▶ This is Polly. It's about our visit to the exhibition this afternoon. I'm not feeling well, so I'm afraid I'll have to _____ (it).

call it off

1 This is Bob speaking. I need my pocket calculator. Can I have it back tomorrow? I can't _____ (it).

2 Hello, Barbara speaking. My train will be arriving at about three-thirty this afternoon. Can you _____ (me)?

3 This is Mike. It's about your offer of the free tickets for the football match. Janet would love to go, so I'd like to _____ (you) (it).

4 Hello, Tom speaking. Jenny said you're coming to Bristol on Thursday. If you'd like to stay with us, we can easily _____ (you).

5 This is John. I've got some good news about the job I applied for at the research laboratory. They're going to _____ (me).

→

6 This is Jim. Dad's leaving for New York tomorrow morning. Would you like to come with me to the airport to _____ (him)?

7 This is your neighbour from the flat below. I'm ringing to complain about your loud music. It _____ (me) half the night!

8 Hi! This is Liz. I'd like to _____ (you) in return for the favour you did me. Would you like to come to the theatre with me?

9 This is Sue speaking. We need more people to help with the party arrangements on Friday. Can we _____ (you)?

10 Hello, this is Jeff. It's about the jazz concert tonight. I'll _____ (you) at seven-thirty. Be ready!

B

Now tell the class what all the callers wanted, as in the example. Include the phrasal verb in your answers.

▶ Polly rang up. She called off our visit to the exhibition this afternoon.

33 ROLE REVERSAL: STAY-AT-HOME FATHERS

Study the phrasal verbs and their meanings, then read the text carefully.

be up against something (3)	be opposed by or confronted with something
bring someone up (4)	rear a child
carry on (1)	continue (EI 110)
cope with something (2)	manage or handle something adequately
get on with something (3)	make progress with something
give up something (4)	stop doing something or leave something, e.g. one's job
help out (1)	give help when needed
look after someone (2)	take care of someone; be responsible for caring for someone
stand up to something (3)	resist something
take off (1)	become popular or successful (EI 147)
turn out	result; prove to be (EI 152)

The phrasal verbs used in the original text have been replaced by the words and phrases in *italics*. Put the text in its original form by putting back the phrasal verbs in their correct form, as in the example. Some are used more than once.

Stay-at-home fathers

Role reversal has not really *become popular* (**taken off**). Couples who swap roles are still few and far between[1]. Is that because women are better at (1) *rearing* children? Or are men just afraid to (2) *resist* tradition?

'The isolation[2] was the worst thing', says Andrew Timpson, who (3) *left* teaching to (4) *take care of* his home and children for two and a half years.

The idea of swapping[3] roles – for the father to stay at home while mum goes out to work – is still a relatively new one. In the 70s it sounded like a great idea. Let the newly liberated woman (5) *make progress with* her career while the New Man stays at home and (6) *takes care of* the house and children.

Now, 10 years or so later, it seems as if we were a little premature[4]. A recent report by the Family Policy Studies Centre concludes:

'Despite important social changes, particularly greater female employment, it is still women in families who undertake the great bulk of housework, cooking, child-care and (7) *taking care of* elderly relatives . . . The much hyped[5] New Man remains a rare species.'

Certainly some would argue that a man cannot replace a mother – that mum is the natural homemaker, while dad is the provider. Some men might (8) *give help* with shopping and cooking, but most would do little more. Some men even believe that doing housework is an insult to their masculinity[6]. Others, like Andrew, want to stay at home – but with reservations. Andrew, who is now about to return to work, says, 'I don't know that I could have (9) *continued* doing it for the rest of my life. I enjoyed it, but I

do want to support my family and I do want to work. I thought I could (10) *handle* being dependent on Maureen, but it (11) *proved* to be tough for both of us.' Maureen says, 'I've got a job I really love. (12) *Continuing* working has allowed me to fulfil my potential[7].'

For many couples who swap roles, traditional attitudes are a major problem. Frank and Joan Roberts found that they (13) *were confronted with* strong views when Frank (14) *left* his job to look after Michael, five, while Joan (15) *continued* with her nursing career. Frank says, 'It is not socially acceptable where we live. People here are (16) *reared* to believe that the man goes out to work and the woman stays at home.'

---

[1] rare   [2] loneliness   [3] exchanging   [4] early   [5] praised; talked about   [6] being a man
[7] what someone is capable of

⟶

Talking point

1   Do you think that women are more naturally suited to bringing up children than men?
2   Do you like looking after children?
3   Are you used to looking after children?
4   What do you think about men and women who give up their jobs to look after their children?
5   Could role reversal take off in your country? If you don't think so, say why. Are your reasons the same as the ones stated in the text?
6   Would you give up a job to look after a child or would you try to carry on working? Consider the advantages and the disadvantages.

34   DO YOU WORK FOR A JERK?

Jerk is a word more common in American than British English. It means 'fool; stupid or unreasonable person'. Another example of American usage in this exercise is *raise*, meaning 'pay rise; increase in salary'.

Study these phrasal verbs and their meanings, then read the extract from *Never Work for a Jerk*.

bottle something up (4)	suppress emotion/anger/worries
break down (1)	fail; come to nothing (EI 107)
bring something up (4)	mention something; introduce something for discussion
carry someone away (4)	overwhelm; fill someone with emotion/enthusiasm
come across (1)	be (clearly) understood
deal with someone/ something (2)	handle or tackle someone/ something (EI 114)
find out (1)	get to know; learn by asking
go on (1)	happen; take place (EI 124)
go over something (2)	rehearse or repeat something (EI 124)
put something off (4)	postpone or delay something
wind up (1) (informal)	finish; end

The phrasal verbs used in the original text have been replaced by the words and phrases in *italics*. Put the text into its original form by putting back the 14 phrasal verbs originally used, in their correct form, as in the example. (Note that one phrasal verb is used twice and one is used three times.)

[1] method of doing something
[2] sound, realistic
[3] foresee, expect
[4] keep
[5] exact, precise
[6] aim, purpose
[7] put into context
[8] too long
[9] uncomplicated, simple
[10] normal and expected
[11] it's your responsibility
[12] says no
[13] work against

Practice makes perfect

If you're having problems with a difficult boss, first of all you need to talk to her. She may not know you are having trouble. By *postponing* (**putting off**) such a meeting while (1) *suppressing* your feelings, you could (2) *be understood* as an irrational person when you finally confront her. No one, least of all management, wants to listen to hysterical complaints.

Before you speak with your supervisor, prepare your approach.[1] Make sure your requests are valid.[2] For example, if you want a bigger office, (3) *get to know* whether one is actually available. Are your expectations realistic? Try to anticipate[3] any objections your boss may (4) *introduce for discussion*. Think positive. (5) *Rehearse* the meeting in your mind and anticipate how your boss will react. Plan how you'll (6) *handle* negative responses, so you can maintain[4] a positive attitude overall.

Be very specific[5] about what you want. For example, 'better communication' is not a clear objective.[6] Neither is merely wanting a raise. If you ask for a raise and your boss says yes, you may (7) *end* with $1.50 more a week. A little background is probably necessary to frame[7] your problem, but don't get (8) *overwhelmed* with long-winded[8] speeches.

Use all the communication skills you have to get the best response from your boss.

Use the most straightforward[9] methods you can in (9) *handling* your boss.

Come out of the meeting with a plan of action. Set a date for another conference, and make these meetings seem like business as usual.[10] If you call a meeting only when something (10) *fails*, you'll be seen as a complainer.

Your boss's reactions

Your boss may be sincerely surprised by the difficulties you (11) *mention for discussion*. It's up to you[11] to explain clearly and calmly just what the problem is.

Even if your boss resists[12] in a straightforward manner, try to (12) *handle* his response. Ask the boss why he objects. Some bosses will use passive resistance. Counter[13] this type of resistance by calling polite attention to it:

'You keep (13) *delaying* the reorganization we discussed. I sense that you don't really want to do it.' This may get you what you want. At the very least it will show the boss that you know what's (14) *happening*. And remember, if nothing seems to work, and your boss really is a jerk, take positive action. Start looking now for a better job.

35 WHEN WOULD YOU SAY THAT?

First, study the phrasal verbs and their meanings.

call for something (2)	demand or justify something (EI 110)
crop up (1)	happen unexpectedly; be mentioned or occur in conversation. (Also **come up**, EI 113)
feel up to something (3)	feel capable of something physically or mentally
get over something (2)	recover from something (illness, shock, disappointment)
jump at something (2) (informal)	accept an offer, etc. with enthusiasm
let on (1) (informal)	reveal something secret against someone's wishes
rush into something (2)	decide to do something too quickly without considering the consequences
see someone out (4)	accompany someone outside or to the door
see to something (2)	attend to something (EI 141)
stick to something (2)	adhere to something; not change something (a story, a plan)
think something over (4)	consider something carefully

Write a short dialogue showing a typical situation in which you would make the following remarks or comments, as in the example.

▷ Something cropped up.

A: 'Why didn't you come to the party? We were all expecting you.'

B: 'I'm sorry. I couldn't come after all. **Something cropped up.**'

1 Sorry, I don't feel up to it.
2 Don't worry. You'll get over it.
3 Whatever happens, I'm going to stick to it.
4 I'll see you out.
5 That calls for a celebration.
6 I would jump at the chance.
7 Don't rush into it!
8 I'll see to it immediately.
9 I promise I won't let on.
10 I'll think it over.

Test exercise 5

(Exercises 29–35)

Complete the sentences with the appropriate phrasal verb in its correct form.

get through
hang up
hold on
count on someone
let someone down
think something over
walk out on someone
get someone down
look up to someone
turn something down
call for someone
call something off
see someone off
take someone on
take someone up on
  something
carry on
cope with someone/
  something
turn out
crop up
feel up to something

1 I've made you a good offer, so _____ (it) and let me have your decision tomorrow.

2 I was talking to Jeff on the phone when suddenly he _____. I've no idea why.

3 I'm very tired. Joan invited me to dinner at her house, but I don't _____ (it). I shall go to bed early.

4 We didn't like John when we first met him, but he has _____ to be a good friend to us.

5 Don't let me disturb you. Please just _____ as if I weren't here.

6 I'm sorry I'm late. Something urgent _____ at the office, so I couldn't leave early.

7 The children are getting very difficult to manage. Sometimes I simply can't _____ (them).

8 I applied for a part-time job at the supermarket. They're going to _____ (me).

9 I've been trying to phone my sister in Australia for over an hour, but I can't _____.

10 'I'm going to the library.' 'If you _____, I'll get the car and drive you there.'

11 Liz promised to help Tony with the report, but she _____ (him) so he had to write it without her.

12 What made Pete _____ his family and his job? Where did he go and why?

13 Sue says that her financial worries are beginning to _____ (her). She's very depressed.

14 You can't possibly say no to such a wonderful job offer. It's too good to _____.

15 We can't have a party with just five people. We'll have to _____ (it).

16 What time is your train? I'll come to the station to _____ (you).

17 Kate has made a great success of her life. We all _____ (her).

18 I'll _____ (you) at seven this evening. Will you be ready by then?

19 I promised Bill that I would lend him some money. He's _____ (me), so I can't disappoint him.

20 Liz made me an offer of £350 for my car. I need the money, so I'm going to _____ (her)(it).

36   STUDY HABITS

Are you a hard-working student?

Study these phrasal verbs and their meanings, then use them in your answers to the questions, as in the example.

catch up (with something) (1,3)	bring oneself/one's work up to date; finish what was not done
come across something (2)	find something by chance
fall behind (with something) (1,3)	be behind/too slow with a schedule; fail to complete something on time
finish something off (4)	complete something
get on (with something) (1,3)	make progress with something (EI 120)
give up (1)	lose interest and admit defeat
go over something (2)	check/examine something again (EI 124)
keep at something (2)	persevere with something
look something up (4)	search for information in a book, etc.
put something off (4)	postpone/delay something
settle down to something (3)	apply oneself to or concentrate on doing something
write something down (4)	write/put something on paper

▶ Do you ever put off doing your work?

Sometimes. But then I fall behind.

I try not to put work off too often, because it is hard to catch up.

Not often. I try to get on with it as soon as possible.

1   What do you do if you fall behind with your work?
2   If you come across an English word that you don't understand, what do you usually do?
3   How do you try to learn and remember new English words?
4   Have you come across any new words today?
5   If you have a difficult problem with your work, do you give up easily?

6   If you have a lot of homework to do, do you settle down to it straightaway?
7   If you have a long exercise to do, do you keep at it until it's finished?
8   How do you check your work for mistakes?
9   If a piece of written homework was only half done, what would you do before your next lesson?
10   What do you usually do if you find an exercise difficult?

37 ASK MAGGIE!

Study these phrasal verbs and their meanings.

break something off (4)	bring something to an abrupt end
bring something up (4)	introduce something for discussion
fall for someone (2) (informal)	be romantically infatuated with someone; be attracted to someone
get at someone (2) (informal)	criticize someone, possibly without cause (EI 119)
get on (with someone) (1,3)	have a good relationship (with someone) (EI 120)
let someone down (4)	disappoint someone
put someone down (4)	speak badly of someone
put someone off (4)	keep someone waiting for an answer/decision/explanation, etc. (EI 137)
send away for something (3)	request or buy something by post
take someone in (4)	trick or cheat someone
talk someone round (4)	persuade someone to do something that he is against. (Also **get round someone**, EI 121)
turn something down (4)	refuse something

→

Here are some letters to *Maggie's Problem Page*.

Gloria S.

Dear Maggie,
I am 18 and have a steady boyfriend, but the trouble is that I have fallen for our new maths teacher. I do

Janet S.

Dear Maggie,
My boyfriend lied to me about a large amount of money. Every time I bring the matter up, he puts me off. I don't want to believe that he stole it but

Michael M.

Dear Maggie,
I don't get on with the other boys in my class. The trouble is that I don't enjoy the things they all like. They play football

Sally R.

Dear Maggie,
Our office manager has invited me to a party. I turned the invitation down. He is trying to talk me round and I don't know what

Jean C.

Dear Maggie,
My best friend has let me down badly, although we have known each other for over

Mark W.

Dear Maggie,
I quarrelled with my fiancée and she broke off our engagement. I've tried to talk her round, but she won't see things my way. I think she's behaving foolishly.

Roger L.

Dear Maggie
I have proposed to my girlfriend four times but she keeps putting me off. I am over thirty and she is only twenty.

Marjorie B.

Dear Maggie,
I sent away for some goods and paid in advance. They haven't arrived after 2 months and I'm starting to believe that I have been taken in. What shall I

Sarah O.

Dear Maggie,
Our head of department is always getting at me. She puts me down in front of other people, although I have never given her real cause for complaint.

A
Now read the letters
carefully, then say whether
the statements are true or
false, as in the examples.

▶ Mark has tried to persuade his girlfriend to change her mind
about their engagement.   **True**

Janet's boyfriend has answered all her questions about a money
matter.   **False**

1 Gloria doesn't like her new maths teacher.
2 Janet has tried to discuss a money matter with her boyfriend
   several times.
3 Michael is popular with the boys in his class because he's a good
   football player.
4 Jean's best friend has disappointed her.
5 Sally has accepted an invitation to a party.
6 Sally's boss is trying to persuade her to change her mind about
   the party.

B
Pretend you have a
problem. Write a letter to
Maggie about it, using as
many of the phrasal verbs
as possible.

7 Mark's girlfriend has said that she won't marry him.
8 Roger's girlfriend has said that she will marry him.
9 Marjorie ordered some goods by post.
10 Marjorie may have been cheated.
11 Sarah's boss often praises her.
12 Sarah's boss complains about her to others.

38 PROFILE OF BRUCE SPRINGSTEEN

Study the phrasal verbs
and nominalized forms
and their meanings.

breakthrough (n)	sudden major success
break up (1)	come to an end; dissolve (EI 108)
call someone up (4)	summon someone for military service (EI 110)
draw something up (4)	prepare a plan, an agreement, etc. (often in writing) (EI 115)
get on with someone (3)	have a good relationship with someone
give something away (4)	give something as a present (EI 122)
give up something (4)	stop doing something
grow up (1)	spend one's childhood years; become adult
keep on (1)	continue

sell-out (n)	performance for which all tickets are sold
sign someone up (4)	give someone a work contract
turn out (1)	result; prove to be (EI 152)

A

Now complete the facts about Bruce Springsteen by putting in the missing phrasal verbs in their correct form, as in the example. Use some twice.

▷   His concert tours are total **sell-outs**, his albums instant hits.

1   Born on September 23, 1949, the son of Irish-Italian parents, he _____ in the run-down town of Freehold, New Jersey.

2   At eight years old he started taking guitar lessons, but hated them so much that he decided to _____ (them).

3   At school he had few friends and didn't _____ the nuns who taught him.

4   He was so unpopular at college that his fellow students _____ a petition asking him to leave.

5   At 16 he won an audition with a record company and was _____.

6   Over the next few years he played with several bands, then formed the Bruce Springsteen Band, which _____ a short while later.

7   By then he had been _____ to fight in Vietnam, but escaped conscription when injured in a motorbike accident.

8   His _____ came in 1975. His record *Born to Run* was a massive success in America.

9   It wasn't until 1985 that he became popular in Britain with the record *Dancing in the Dark*. His tour in Britain later that year was a _____.

10   In the past two years alone, he has _____ nearly £2 million to help the poor, homeless and jobless in every town he plays.

11   Five years ago, feeling the full isolation of being a star, he almost _____ (it all).

12   Of his wife he says: 'Julianne has _____ to be the one thing that was missing in my life.'

13   Now, with every record he releases going straight into the charts, it seems as if Springsteen really was born to run and _____ running . . .

B

Imagine you are going to interview a pop star or a pop group. Think up some questions to ask him/her/them using **grow up, sign up, break up, give up something, sell-out, breakthrough**. Now work in pairs. One partner is the interviewer, the other is the pop star. Hold an interview using the questions you have prepared. Then reverse roles.

39   SITUATIONS

Study these phrasal verbs and their meanings, then use them to say what you would probably do in a given situation, as in the example.

What would you do?

call something off (4)	cancel something
join in (1)	participate in something that is taking place
jump at something (2) (informal)	accept an offer, etc. with enthusiasm
look someone up (4)	pay an informal visit to someone living in another town or to someone you haven't seen for a long time
move out (1)	vacate a house, room, etc.
own up (to something) (1, 3)	confess or admit (something)
pick something up (4)	take or go to get something (EI 135)
send for someone (2)	call someone to your house for help
take someone up on something (6)	accept an offer from someone (EI 149)
think something over (4)	consider something carefully
turn something down (4)	reject or refuse something

▷ You receive an invitation to a party, but you don't really want to go.

I would think it over.

I would probably turn the invitation down.

1   Someone in your family is ill and you don't know what to do.
2   You make a mistake at work and you think someone else may be blamed for it.
3   You have received a job offer with good pay, but you think the job may be boring.
4   You see a £5 note lying on a bus seat. No one claims it.
5   You arrive at a party where people are dancing and having fun.
6   You are having trouble with your landlady. The room is expensive and not very comfortable.
7   A friend makes you a very good offer for your old car.

→

8 You have the chance of going to England for a year to study English. You would like to go, but your family may object.
9 You are travelling to New York next week. You have a friend who lives there.
10 You have invited some friends to a barbecue, but on the day it rains heavily.

Talking point

1 Have you ever turned down a job? What were your reasons?
2 When was the last time you looked up an old friend? Was he/she pleased to see you?
3 Have you ever had to call off something important, for example, your holiday plans, a birthday party, a special celebration, a meeting, etc? Why?
4 When was the last time that someone took you up on an offer? What did you offer to do?

40 GIVING UP SMOKING

These two articles from weekly magazines give advice on how to give up smoking.

Study the phrasal verbs and their meanings.

calm someone down (4)	make someone feel calm and relaxed
cut down on something (3)	reduce one's consumption of something
fall into something (2)	be divided into something (groups/categories/parts, etc.)
get on with something (3)	make progress with something
get up (1)	stand up (EI 122)
give something away (4)	give something as a present (EI 122)
give up (1)	stop
give up something (4)	stop doing something one enjoys
light up (1)	light a cigarette

pack something in (4) (informal)	stop doing something; renounce something (EI 134)
run out of something (3)	use all one has of something; have no more of something
settle down to something (3)	apply oneself to or concentrate on something
take up something (4)	begin to pursue something as an interest/hobby
washing-up (n)	the washing of dishes and cutlery after a meal

Now read the articles carefully and put in the missing phrasal verbs in their correct form, as in the example. Note that some phrasal verbs are used more than once.

Yes, you *can* give up smoking if you try

'No, thanks, I don't smoke.' If you are really addicted to smoking and want to **give up**, that may be the hardest sentence you ever have to say. 'I don't smoke' has to become an attitude of mind[1]; there is no short-cut to __1__ smoking and your most powerful weapon is your own will-power.

There are four steps to __2__ smoking:

1 Thinking about your reasons for stopping,
2 Preparing to stop: this means getting rid of[2] any secret stores of cigarettes and your lighter, washing ashtrays and __3__ (them), and arranging to do things which prevent you from smoking. __4__ swimming or other sports, see non-smoking friends more often and go to places where smoking isn't allowed – the theatre, for example. Above all, practise __5__ the number of cigarettes you smoke every day. Start smoking later each day. Ban rooms in your house in which you allow yourself to smoke, starting with the bathroom, kitchen and bedroom. Allow yourself to __6__ cigarettes now and again. Don't ever buy more than one pack at a time.
3 Stopping: on the day you stop, arrange to do lots of things you enjoy. Don't just sit there thinking how much you want a cigarette; __7__ and do something positive, even if it's the __8__. __9__ a hobby such as knitting, gardening or carpentry[3] in which you use your hands.
4 Staying stopped: this is the hardest part, particularly if you have been a heavy smoker. You may well feel depressed, irritable, anxious, or suffer from cramps or headaches. But remember that withdrawal symptoms only last a few weeks. Wanting to __10__ is your best asset[4] and in the end, if your motivation is high enough, you will succeed in beating nicotine rather than letting it beat you.'

[1] way of thinking
[2] throwing away
[3] woodwork
[4] plus point, advantage

→

Packing it in – the no-puff kit[5] for young smokers

For kids who find __11__ smoking a real drag[6], help is at hand. All they have to do is ask.

The questions and answers are in a new kit called __12__ (*it*). Targeted[7] at 15- to 20-year-olds, it's been produced by Dr Anne Charlton, Director of the Cancer Research Campaign Education and Child Studies Research Group.

Dr Charlton's kit is the result of three years of research into the smoking habits of young people, and it aims to help them kick[8] the habit by getting them to analyse the reasons *why* they smoke.

'When they have decided why they smoke, they use their own plan in the kit to help __13__ (it).'

According to Dr Charlton the young smokers __14__ the following categories:

* The automatic smoker.
* The social confidence smoker, who smokes at parties, for example.
* The confidence smoker – the person who feels cigarettes give him confidence to do things.
* The pleasure smoker, who finds smoking creates a sociable, friendly feeling in company.
* The concentration smoker – the person who __15__ before __16__ work or study, thinking it __17__ (him).
* The comfort smoker who believes that smoking makes him feel better.
* The sensation smoker, who likes the feel of a cigarette in the hand.
* The keep-going smoker. Someone who is bored – in a dull job perhaps – and needs a boost to __18__ (it).

'At 15 there are very few people who are addicted to cigarettes, but they could very easily be hooked[9] by the time they reach 20.'

[5] information pack
[6] difficulty, problem
[7] aimed
[8] stop completely
[9] addicted

Talking point

1   What advice does the first article give to smokers? Do you think it is good advice?

2   According to the second article, who is 'the concentration smoker', and who is 'the keep-going smoker'?

3   Have you ever tried to give up smoking? Why were you or were you not successful?

4   Do you know anyone who has given it up successfully? How did they do it?

41 HOW SELF-CONFIDENT ARE YOU?

Do you panic at the thought of public speaking? Or do you enjoy it? To find out how shy or how self-confident you are, do the following quiz.

First, study these phrasal verbs and their meanings.

answer back (1)	return a criticism in a rude manner
blow up (1)	suddenly become angry (EI 106)
break in (1)	interrupt someone who is speaking (EI 107)
brush something aside (4)	disregard something as unimportant
call on someone (2)	visit someone
get on (with someone) (1,3)	have a good relationship (with someone) (EI 120)
get out of something (3)	avoid having to do something
give up (1)	lose interest and admit defeat
go along with something (3)	agree or comply with something (EI 123)
push in (1)	push in front of someone (e.g. in a queue)
push off (1) (informal)	leave; go away. (Also **clear off**, EI 111)
sit out (1)	not participate in an activity
stick up for someone (3)	defend someone
warm up (1)	become lively and relaxed

Now do the quiz.

Score as follows:

almost always 1
sometimes   2
rarely   3
never   4

1 If someone criticizes you, do you stick up for yourself?
2 Do you get on well with strangers?
3 At meetings or discussions do you break in if you have something important to say?
4 If someone is wasting your time, would you politely tell him or her to push off?
5 If someone you hardly know invited you to call on him or her, would you do so?
6 If you're angry with someone, do you blow up?
7 If someone is rude to you, do you answer back?

$\longrightarrow$

Now score like this:

never	1
rarely	2
sometimes	3
almost always	4

8 If someone pays you a compliment, do you prefer to brush it aside?

9 In a group, do you prefer to go along with other people's suggestions rather than make your own?

10 Do you sit out while others enjoy themselves?

11 Do you give up easily when you feel challenged?

12 At a party or social gathering, does it take you a long time to warm up?

13 In a shop, etc., do you let others push in even if it's your turn?

14 Do you try to get out of doing things that make you the centre of attention, e.g. public speaking?

Add up your score and look up your self-confidence rating in the key!

Talking point

Did you answer the questions honestly? Did you think you would be more or less self-confident and why? Discuss with other students whether they think your self-confidence rating is accurate. Ask other students the quiz questions.

Test exercise 6

(Exercises 36–41)

Complete the sentences with the appropriate phrasal verb in its correct form.

catch up with something
fall behind
give up
keep at something
settle down to
    something
fall for someone
get at someone
take someone in
talk someone round
keep on
join in
look someone up
own up
get on with something
pack something in
brush something aside
get out of something
go along with something
push in
stick up for someone

1   You have almost solved the crossword puzzle. You mustn't _____ now!

2   I was ill for two weeks, so I've _____ with my work.

3   I have a report to finish before I can _____ watching television.

4   It isn't that woman's turn. It's yours. Don't let her _____.

5   I have already told Joe that I won't go to Spain with him, but he's still trying to _____ (me).

6   Simon _____ an Irish girl that he met on holiday. Three months later they were married!

7   This painting can't possibly be an original. I think we've been _____.

8   I've asked Jeff several times not to smoke in the bedroom, but he _____ doing it.

9   I wish the boss would stop _____ (me). I haven't done anything wrong.

10 I've been working hard on the report. If I _____ (it), I shall finish it by this evening.

11 Terry doesn't like his new job. He's only had it for three months, but he's already decided to _____ (it).

12 Don't waste time chatting! _____ your essay!

13 We're moving to Liverpool next month. Remember to _____ (us) if you're in the area.

14 You promised to make a speech at Jill's wedding, so you can't _____ (it) now. Jill would be disappointed.

15 The teacher asked the pupils who had broken the chair, but at first no one _____.

16 'How did you get the black eye?' 'My friend was in a fight, so I _____ (him) and got hit too.'

17 You say that Margaret's suggestion is good, so does that mean you are going to _____ (it)?

18 Some students were sitting round a camp fire singing songs. They asked me to _____, so I did.

19 He ignored my request. He simply _____ (it) as if he hadn't heard what I said.

20 I've been away from home for a month, so now I want to _____ the news. What's been happening?

42   FRIENDS

What are the characteristics of a good friend?

Study these phrasal verbs and their meanings.

help someone out (4)	help someone to overcome a difficulty
hold out on someone (3) (informal)	deliberately not tell someone something; keep information from someone on purpose
lead someone on (4)	mislead someone; try to persuade or encourage someone to do or believe something
let someone down (4)	disappoint someone
look down on someone (3)	regard someone as inferior
pick on someone (2)	criticize someone without reason
play up to someone (3) (informal)	flatter someone to gain an advantage
see someone through (something) (4, 5)	help someone through a difficult situation, etc.
set someone up (4) (informal)	make someone appear guilty (EI 142)
stand by someone (2)	support and comfort someone
stand up for someone (3)	defend someone
turn on someone (2)	criticize someone sharply; attack someone

Do you agree or disagree with the statements below? Begin your answer with 'Yes' or 'No', as in the examples, and use the appropriate phrasal verb.

▶   A good friend is . . .

. . . someone who helps you to overcome a difficulty.
Yes, a good friend helps you out.

. . . someone who disappoints you.
No, a good friend doesn't let you down.

1   . . . someone who misleads you.
2   . . . someone who keeps information from you on purpose.
3   . . . someone who supports and comforts you.
4   . . . someone who regards you as inferior.
5   . . . someone who flatters you to gain an advantage.
6   . . . someone who makes you appear guilty.
7   . . . someone who defends you.
8   . . . someone who attacks you sharply.

9   . . . someone who criticizes you without reason.
10   . . . someone who helps you through a difficult situation.

Talking point

Think about the phrasal verbs used in the exercise and say which three qualities you think are most important in a friend or partner. How do you try to be a good friend?

43   TALKING ABOUT SPORT

Study these phrasal verbs and their meanings.

build something up (4)	develop or increase something gradually
come up against something (3)	be confronted with a difficulty or problem
do without something (2)	manage without something one wants or usually has (EI 115)
get up to something (3)	reach the standard or level of something (EI 122)
give up something (4)	stop (doing/having) something you enjoy
go in for something (3)	participate or compete in something (EI 124)
go through with something (3)	continue something to the end
keep up something (4)	continue doing something regularly
look on (1)	watch inactively
opt out (1)	choose not to do something or to stop doing something
pay off (1)	prove to be profitable
settle for something (2)	be prepared to accept something
stick to something (2)	adhere to or persevere with something
take up something (4)	begin to pursue a hobby/sport/interest (EI 149)
work out (1)	do physical fitness and health training exercises

⟶

Read the text then answer the questions.

Most of us are interested in one kind of sport or another, even if we don't *go in for* it actively. Lots of people *take up* a particular sport at an early age, for example tennis, skiing or ice-skating. If they get up to a suitably high standard, they may go in for local competitions or even championships. But special training is hard work and most young people don't keep it up. Many of them opt out when they come up against tough competition.

To become a professional in any sport, you have to go through with a strict training schedule. And it's not easy! It means doing without some of life's little pleasures, too. For example, to build up your physical strength you may have to stick to a special diet and give up some of your favourite foods. Smoking and alcohol are out, and to keep fit you have to work out regularly every day.

Sometimes it all pays off, but the road to success is long and there are no guarantees. No wonder that countless young talents decide to settle for a regular job instead, and, as far as professional sport is concerned, prefer to look on as spectators.

1   The first two phrasal verbs in the text are given in *italics*. Can you find 14 more? Write them down in the order they appear.
2   What do they mean? Replace each phrasal verb with a word or phrase with the same meaning, as in the examples.

▶   *go in for*

participate in

take up

begin to pursue

Talking point

1   Did you take up any sport as a child? What made you take it up?
2   Did you keep it up? If not, why not?
3   Have you given up a sport in recent years? If so, why did you give it up? (e.g. too expensive, not enough time, no partner, lack of facilities, for health reasons)
4   Do you ever go in for competitions or championships?
5   In your opinion, what are the different reasons why people take up a sport? (e.g. health, social contacts, prestige)
6   Do you know anyone who goes in for an unusual kind of sport? (e.g. mountaineering, hang-gliding, ski-jumping, deep-sea diving)

44   ON THE ROAD

Phrasal verbs are often used when talking about driving.

Study these phrasal verbs and their meanings.

back out (1)	reverse a vehicle out of a garage, parking place, etc.
break down (1)	stop functioning because of a mechanical fault (EI 107)
change down (1)	change a vehicle into a lower gear
cut in (1)	drive sharply in front of another car when overtaking (EI 113)
cut out (1)	(engine, etc.) suddenly stop functioning
draw up (1)	come to a stop at the side of the road, at someone's house, etc.
drive off (1)	begin to move; drive away
hold something up (4)	delay or stop something (EI 127)
pull out (1)	(vehicle) move out of a line of traffic, parking place, junction, etc. (EI 136)
pull up (1)	(vehicle) halt; stop
run into something (2)	drive into something and cause an accident
slow down (1)	reduce speed
speed up (1)	increase speed
turn off (1)	drive right or left at a junction or crossroads

A

Now look carefully at the traffic situations in the pictures on the next page and use suitable phrasal verbs to complete the sentences as in the example.

Car A is _____.

Car A is driving off/pulling out.

1   Car B is _____.

2   Car C is _____.

3   The tractor is _____ the traffic.

4   The sportscar has _____ a tree.

5   Car D has _____.

6   The delivery van has just _____.

7   The motorbike has just _____ dangerously.

8   The lorry is _____.

9   All the traffic has to _____.

B
Complete the sentences
with the correct phrasal
verb.

1 If the car engine suddenly stops functioning, we say it has ____.
pulled up   slowed down   cut out

2 If your car won't go we say it has ____.
drawn up   broken down   broken up

3 If you put your car from fourth gear into third gear you ____.
break down   change down   pull up

4 ____ means 'go faster'.
draw up   speed up   pull up

5 ____ means 'stop your car'.
draw up   hold up   change up

45   A TRUE STORY

Study the phrasal verbs
and their meanings.

break down (1)	lose emotional control because of shock, grief, etc. (EI 107)
break up (1)	come to an end; dissolve (EI 108)
call someone in (4)	request someone's services; ask for someone's professional help
carry on (1)	continue
come in (1)	be earned; be received as income (EI 112)
end up (1)	finally be somewhere or do something; finish (as)
give in to something (3)	surrender or yield to something
give up something (4)	stop doing something one enjoys; stop indulging in something
go on (1)	1 take place; happen 2 continue (EI 124)
go through something (2)	suffer pain, hardship, loss (EI 125)
go without something (2)	not have something one usually has
make something out (4)	write a bill, cheque, etc. (EI 132)

⟶

roll in (1)　　　　　come in large quantities
　　　　　　　　　　　(EI 139)

take something in (4)　fully understand something
　　　　　　　　　　　(EI 147)

take off (1)　　　　begin to improve/be
　　　　　　　　　　　successful/make a profit
　　　　　　　　　　　(EI 147)

walk out (1)　　　　leave and not return

A

In this true story, parts of the phrasal verbs used in the original text are missing. Can you put them back in, as in the examples? Use two phrasal verbs twice.

When Sue Reardon's jet set[1] life with snooker[2] champion Ray broke **up,** she never imagined that she would **end** up in court, like a common thief.

When my marriage to this rich, celebrated[3] man ended, I couldn't give ___1___ the luxurious[4] lifestyle that we'd once so enjoyed together. My husband's relationship with a younger woman had apparently been going ___2___ for some time. He confessed to me – over the telephone. My mind went back over the years we'd shared together. I had been ___3___ so much with him, right from the early days when he was a miner and then a policeman. With Ray's first snooker win we had bought a bungalow.

Life as a professional player really took ___4___ for him. Those were the days[5] – travelling to Tenerife one week, Canada the next. I thought nothing of[6] spending £500 on a dress and buying six pairs of shoes at a time.

After Ray walked ___5___ money stopped coming ___6___. But I ___7___ on buying nice things.

In the divorce settlement[7] I got the house and £1,500 a month. It may sound a lot, but I was already £6,000 in debt[8]. At Christmas that year I shopped as usual. I didn't see why my daughter should go ___8___ the nice things she'd been used to. So the bills went ___9___ growing . . . and growing.

I ended ___10___ cleaning five mornings a week for a businessman for £38. Then one day, about three months after I'd started to work for him, I slipped one of his cigarette lighters and a watch into my pocket. I hid them at home. It was like hiding my guilt.

[1] exciting
[2] a game similar to pool or billiards
[3] famous
[4] very comfortable
[5] i.e. the days of pleasure
[6] didn't stop to think about
[7] agreement
[8] had unpaid bills of £6,000

By New Year's Eve I had just £14 left. I knew £200 in cash was sitting in a drawer at work, so I took it.

A few weeks later I spotted[9] £1,350 worth of cheques made __11__ to my boss's son. I changed the name and paid them into my own account. I __12__ down when I'd done it, but the bills from Christmas were __13__ in and I was absolutely desperate for cash.

My debts were a terrible burden, but the guilt I felt was even worse. So I went over to my boss's house and confessed.[10]

The police were __14__ in and they searched my home from top to bottom.[11]

The next thing I knew I was in court, pleading guilty. After I left the court room I couldn't eat or sleep for a week. The magistrates[12] ordered me to repay the money and pay the court costs. I'm doing that at the moment, but even now I still can't take __15__ all that has happened – it seems like a nightmare.[13] All the rich and famous friends I made while I was with Ray have abandoned me.

The important thing now is to put my life back together again, helped by the love of my two children. If there's one thing I hope people understand, it's that I'm not a wicked woman. I just gave __16__ to temptation.

[9] saw/noticed
[10] admitted my crime
[11] thoroughly
[12] court officials/legal officials
[13] very bad dream

B

Now answer these questions. In your answers use the phrasal verbs from the text.

1 When did Sue Reardon's troubles begin?
2 When did the money stop coming in?
3 Was she able to adapt to the change?
4 Did she think only of herself?
5 How did she try to deal with her debts in an honest manner?
6 What made her steal?
7 What did she do with the cheques?
8 How did she feel immediately afterwards?
9 Did she fully understand what was happening to her?
10 She says she's not a wicked woman. What explanation does she give for her actions?

Test exercise 7

(Exercises 42–45)

Complete the sentences with the appropriate phrasal verb in its correct form.

look down on someone
pick on someone
stand up for someone
come up against
  something
pay off
settle for something
break down
draw up
slow down
break up
call someone in
give in to something
go on
make something out
take something in

1   Harry has been training very hard to qualify for the Olympic team. He hopes that the hard work will _____.

2   His condition is worse than before. I think we should _____ a doctor.

3   I was on a diet, but when I saw the chocolate cake I _____ temptation. I couldn't resist it.

4   There's a lot of noise _____ in the flat above. I think they must be moving furniture.

5   A red car has just _____ in front of our house. Are we expecting anyone?

6   I've won a million pounds! I don't believe it! I simply can't _____ (it)!

7   Don't _____ Ted just because he's not as good at the job as you are. You've had more experience.

8   When the teacher accused Tom of having broken a window, Jenny _____ (him), because she knew that Tom hadn't done it.

9   If you _____ any unexpected problems, please let me know immediately.

10 Could you _____, please. I don't like driving so fast on country roads.

11 Janet didn't get a place at university, so she has _____ a job at a bank instead.

12 I'm sorry I'm late. The car has _____ again. I've left it about a mile down the road.

13 The name on the cheque is wrong. The cheque is _____ to your brother, not to you.

14 Alan was very unhappy when his marriage _____ two years ago.

15 I don't know why the boss _____ the new office boy. He's not very bright but he's hard-working and willing to learn.

46 A LIFE IN THE DAY OF CELIA HAMMOND

Celia Hammond, cat lover, talks to *The Sunday Times Magazine*.

First, study the phrasal verbs and their meanings.

come on (1)	begin slowly (EI 112)
dash off (1)	leave in a hurry
deal with something (2)	handle/tackle/solve something (EI 114)
finish up (1)	arrive at a place or end with an action as the result of earlier actions. (Also **end up**, EI 117)
get something off (4)	remove something (e.g. clothing). (Also **take something off**, EI 148)
give up (1)	lose interest and stop trying to do something
give up something (4)	forgo or surrender something
hang around (1) (informal)	wait idly without having anything to do
put someone off something (5)	make someone dislike something
put up with someone/ something (3)	tolerate or bear someone/ something
run off (1)	run away
set something up (4)	establish or open something
take something off (4)	take free time from work (EI 148)
tuck into something (2)	eat something eagerly
turn up (1)	appear; arrive
wake up (1)	stop sleeping; open one's eyes after sleep (EI 152)
work something out (4)	calculate or find the answer to something (EI 153)

⟶

A

Read the text carefully. Parts of the phrasal verbs have been missed out. Can you put them back in in their correct form, as in the example?

Celia Hammond **gave** up a successful modelling career fifteen years ago, to concentrate on saving London's cats. Eighteen months ago she ___1___ up the Celia Hammond Animal Trust.

'The first thing I do when I ___2___ up is ___3___ out where I am. I've usually been out trapping[1] cats the night before and I'm quite likely to have slept on the floor at a friend's house. Then I'll have a quick cup of tea. I don't take vitamins, but I'll have some garlic if I think I've got a cold coming ___4___.

I eat a lot of chocolate and bread, lots of unhealthy things. I met a woman on a bus once who showed me some pictures of a slaughterhouse[2] and it ___5___ me off eating meat, but I still feed the cats with meat. Sometimes I'll go a whole week without a hot meal, just ___6___ into crisps and chocolate bars in the car en route[3] somewhere. I finished ___7___ in hospital once; my weight dropped to seven stone.

As a model I was spoilt rotten[4], because I only worked with the best. I used to go abroad a lot, until Norman Parkinson (a photographer) refused to take me any more because I'd stay out all night feeding stray[5] cats. Next morning I'd ___8___ up with false nails hiding my broken ones, trying to look as if I'd had a good night's sleep. Clothes were never important to me. When you're wearing beautiful clothes all day it's a relief to get them ___9___.

I've spent everything I ever had on saving cats. I don't have a social life. My friends have long since ___10___ up. I never take holidays but I ___11___ two days off at Christmas when I stayed with friends in Wales. In some ways I wish I didn't have this obsession. My life would have been a lot more fun without it. No man is going to put ___12___ with me.

I get a lot of emergency calls that have to be dealt ___13___, like animals being trapped inside a building due for demolition[6]. Concentration is very tiring, especially if you're ___14___ around in some cold, derelict[7] building for four or five hours, waiting for the one cat who chooses to play hard to get. But the majority of the cats I trap are domestic ones who have ___15___ off.

Weekends are always spent finding homes for the cats best suited to rehabilitation[8]. The others go to farms or stables. I visit all the families personally, and I'm never finished until eleven o'clock at night, and that's early.

Sometimes if I'm out at night in the West End[9], where I do a lot of trapping, I see people done up[10], dashing ___16___ to the theatre. Meanwhile there I am lurking[11] in some building site, and I wish things could be different. Just for a second, then it's gone.'

[1] catching
[2] place where animals are killed (for food)
[3] on the way
[4] treated very well
[5] lost, runaway
[6] due to be pulled down
[7] deserted; in need of repair
[8] becoming tame again
[9] the entertainment area of London
[10] wearing evening dress
[11] waiting and hiding

B

Are these statements about
Celia Hammond true or
false?

1   Recently she opened a cats' home.
2   She usually sleeps at home.
3   She takes vitamins to cure a cold.
4   She eats a lot of meat.
5   She often eats crisps and chocolate bars.
6   As a model, she sometimes came to photo sessions looking less than her best.
7   She enjoyed wearing beautiful clothes.
8   She's married.
9   Her friends often contact her.
10 Over Christmas she worked in Wales.

Talking point

Celia Hammond's obsession with cats has changed her life completely. In what ways has her life changed?

47   YOUR HOROSCOPE

Horoscopes are full of phrasal verbs.

Study these phrasal verbs
and their meanings.

call something off (4)	cancel something
call on someone (2)	visit someone (EI 110)
come off (1)	materialize; happen (EI 112)
come up against something (3)	be confronted with something
count on someone (2)	rely on someone
crop up (1)	arise unexpectedly. (Also **come up**, EI 113)
drop by (1)	visit; call. (Also **call by**, **call in**, EI 110)
fall in with something (3)	agree with or accept something that others want. (Also **go along with someone/something**, EI 123)
get someone down (4)	depress someone
get on (with someone) (1,3)	have a good relationship (with someone) (EI 120)

→

get over something (2)	recover from a shock or unpleasant surprise (EI 121)
get out of something (3)	avoid having to do something
let someone down (4)	disappoint someone
pile up (1)	accumulate
put something off (4)	postpone or delay something
put up with something (3)	tolerate something
sort something out (4)	solve a problem; put a matter in order
take something on (4)	undertake to do something; accept something
talk someone into something (5)	try to persuade someone to do something
turn something down (4)	refuse or reject something

Aquarius (January 20–February 18)
A difficult situation may begin to get you down mid-week, but be optimistic. Be extra careful on the 12th.

Pisces (February 19–March 20)
A good week for finance and romance. An unpleasant situation may crop up mid-week, but you can count on support from someone close.

Aries (March 21–April 20)
A good week socially. An old friend may call on you at the weekend. Don't let yourself be talked into anything you don't want to do.

Taurus (April 21–May 20)
Someone close may let you down. Don't over-react. You'll soon get over it, so be prepared to forgive and forget. Putting things off is unwise.

Gemini (May 21–June 20)
You will get on with everybody this week, but it would be better to turn down a weekend invitation. Be suspicious of strangers.

Cancer (June 21–July 20)
You may have to put up with some opposition from a member of your family. But be patient and others will fall in with your plans after all.

Leo (July 21–August 21)
You may have to call off some travel arrangements towards the weekend. A surprise meeting mid-week. A successful week at work.

Virgo (August 22–September 22)
A friend may ask for your help in sorting out a problem, but try to avoid difficult situations. A good week for romance.

Libra (September 23–October 22)
Tuesday will be a good day for money matters. You may come up against some opposition mid-week, so be strong-willed.

Scorpio (October 23–November 22)
Something you were looking forward to may not come off, so be prepared. An old friend may drop by at the weekend.

Sagittarius (November 23–December 20)
Personal problems will pile up, but keep calm. Finish what you start on Thursday and Friday. Good news at the weekend.

Capricorn (December 21–January 19)
Be prepared to take on a new task. If you try to get out of it, you may regret it later. An opportunity for travel mid-week.

A

Now that you have read the horoscopes, say whether the statements are true or false, as in the examples.

▶ Aries may have a visitor at the weekend.   **True**
Taurus will be pleasantly surprised by someone close.   **False**

1 Virgo may be asked to solve a problem for a friend.
2 Something disappointing may happen to Scorpio.
3 People won't be very friendly to Gemini this week.
4 Someone may try to persuade Aries to do something against his/her will.
5 Aquarius will enjoy dealing with a difficult situation.
6 Taurus will soon recover from a disappointment.
7 Gemini should accept a weekend invitation.
8 Leo may have to cancel some travel plans.
9 Someone in Cancer's family may oppose his/her plans or wishes.
10 Sagittarius will find himself/herself confronted by many problems.
11 Capricorn should reject new responsibilities.   ⟶

12 Scorpio may have a visitor at the weekend.
13 Pisces may find himself/herself in an unpleasant situation.

B
Invent a horoscope for
yourself for next week,
using as many phrasal
verbs as possible.

14 Taurus should do all the things he/she has to do.
15 People will do what Cancer wants in the end.
16 Capricorn may regret taking on a new task.
17 Pisces shouldn't expect help from friends.
18 Not everyone will agree with what Libra wants to do.

48 HOW IMPULSIVE ARE YOU?

Do you plan your life or are you impulsive? To find out, do the
quiz!

First, study the phrasal
verbs and their meanings.

chew something over (4) (informal)	think about something slowly and carefully
drop in on someone (3)	pay someone a casual visit. (Also **call on someone**, EI 110)
fall in with something (3)	accept a plan; agree with something. (Also **go along with something**, EI 123)
get on with something (3)	make progress with something
give in to something (3)	surrender or yield to something
put something aside (4)	save something for later use
ring back (1)	telephone again later
ring off (1)	end a telephone conversation. (Also **hang up**, EI 126)
rush into something (2)	decide to do something too quickly without considering the consequences
set off (1)	leave home; begin a journey (Also **set out**, EI 142)
set to (1)	start energetically
settle on something (2)	decide on or choose something
sit something out (4)	attend something until the end
sit up (1)	go to bed much later than usual (EI 144)
snap something up (4)	take or buy something eagerly and without hesitation

splash out on something (3)   spend money on something carelessly or lavishly

switch off (1) (informal)   stop paying attention because of lack of interest

try something on (4)   put an item of clothing on to see how it looks (EI 151)

turn something down (4)   reject or refuse something

turn up (1)   appear, arrive

1

If you are planning to do something special, when do you decide what you will wear?

a   Ten minutes before I have to set off.
b   The night before, usually trying on different clothes before deciding.
c   The same morning, but I give myself enough time to settle on something suitable.

2

You meet someone of the opposite sex who attracts you. You make a date with this person. Before the date you find out that he/she is married. Would you . . .

a   give in to temptation and keep the date?
b   ask a friend for advice?
c   simply not turn up?

3

Money matters. Do you . . .

a   put money aside whenever you have extra cash?
b   put a fixed amount aside every week?
c   splash out on luxuries when you have extra cash?

4

Would you describe yourself as . . .

a   a careful shopper who never rushes into buying?
b   someone who snaps up a bargain whatever the cost?
c   a moderately careful shopper?

5

Do you drop in on people unexpectedly?

a   Yes, often.
b   Sometimes.
c   Never.

6

You have a deadline for a project in four weeks' time. Are you likely to . . .

a   set to immediately and finish it two weeks early?
b   wait until week four and sit up every night working?
c   work at a steady pace and finish it on time?

7

At work or school, if you are not in a working mood, you . . .

a   do as little as possible.
b   get on with your work whether you feel like it or not.
c   simply switch off and don't work at all.

8

Have you ever got up and walked out of a play/lecture/concert because you were bored?

a   Never. I sit everything out once I've bought a ticket.
b   Often. I don't believe in wasting time with boring things.
c   Occasionally.

→

9
What do you think about people who phone you at odd times (e.g. very early or very late) just for a chat?

a   I don't mind. I like impulsive, easy-going people.
b   They annoy me. I tell them to ring back at a more convenient time.
c   I don't mind if it happens only occasionally, but I ring off as soon as possible.

10
Some of your friends decide to drive somewhere for the weekend at very short notice. They want you to go with them. You . . .

a   fall in with the plan and say 'Yes' immediately.
b   say you need time to chew it over.
c   turn it down because it's all happening too fast.

Score like this:

	a	b	c			a	b	c
1	5	1	3		6	1	5	3
2	5	3	1		7	3	1	5
3	3	1	5		8	1	5	3
4	1	5	3		9	5	1	3
5	5	3	1		10	5	3	1

Add up your score and look up your rating in the key!

Now work with a partner. Ask each other the quiz questions giving the three alternatives. Try to remember the alternatives and answer without looking at the book if possible. You can answer truthfully or just for fun.

Talking point

Did you answer the questions honestly? Do you think your rating is accurate? Did you think you would be more or less impulsive and why?

Test exercise 8

(Exercises 46–48)

Complete the sentences with the appropriate phrasal verb in its correct form.

come on
put someone off something
turn up
come off
drop by
fall in with something
take something on
drop in on someone
put something aside
ring back
ring off
set to
settle on something
sit up
try something on

1   I wonder if this dress fits. I'll _____ (it) and see.

2   I feel weak and dizzy. It _____ after lunch. Perhaps it's something I ate.

3   The position that the company has offered me carries a lot of responsibility. I'm not sure whether or not I should _____ (it).

4   'Did you enjoy the concert last night with Liz?' 'We didn't go. I waited an hour, but Liz didn't _____.'

5   I'm sorry, but I'll have to _____ now. Someone has just come into the office.

6   Mary rang but she didn't have much time to talk. I told her I would _____ this evening.

7   Don't spend the money you won. Why don't you _____ (it) until you have enough to buy something you really want?

8   If you intend to visit Aunt Pamela, phone her first. She doesn't like people _____ (her) without warning.

9   There was an excellent film on television late last night. We _____ especially to watch it.

10 Why have you suddenly stopped eating fish? What _____ (you) (it)?

11 We couldn't decide whether to book a holiday in Spain or Italy. We finally _____ Spain.

12 You must pay us a visit next time you're in Cambridge. Just _____ any time. There's usually someone at home.

13 Kate had a lot of homework to do today, so she _____ as soon as she came home. She has almost finished it now.

14 'Do you think Henry will _____ our arrangements?' 'Yes. I'm sure he'll agree with everything.'

15 We had plans to go to live in Australia, but they didn't _____. So now we're going to stay here.

Key

PART I

1

1 down   2 off   3 on   4 off   5 on   6 along

2

1 take off   2 slow down   3 coming along
4 hold on   5 get on   6 set off

3

1 hold on   2 coming along   3 get on   4 took off/
set off   5 set off   6 slow down

4

1 into   2 after   3 at   4 with   5 on   6 off

5

1 count on   2 was with   3 takes after   4 went off
5 look into   6 be at

6

1 was at   2 look into   3 count on   4 takes after
5 went off   6 am with

7

1 up   2 for   3 up   4 with   5 up   6 down

8

1 put up with   2 look up to   3 come up with
4 goes in for   5 come up against   6 got down to

9

1 put up with   2 came up against   3 goes in for
4 look up to   5 comes up with   6 get down to

10

1 in   2 off   3 up   4 up   5 down   6 off

11

1 called   2 rang   3 brought   4 take   5 let
6 packing

12

1 let down   2 ring up   3 bring up   4 packing in
5 taking off   6 call off

13

1 Who let him down?   2 When did Jack pack it in?
3 Who brought them up?   4 Who rang her up?
5 When did Mr Jackson call it off?   6 Who can take
them off?

14

1 Who brought the children up?/Who brought up the
children?   2 Who brought up the children who lost
their parents in a car accident?   3 They called the
cricket match off./They called off the cricket match.
4 They called off the cricket match against the team
from Perth.   5 She packed her boring job in./She
packed in her boring job.   6. She packed in a boring
job without prospects.   7 We rang the Robinsons
up./We rang up the Robinsons.   8 We rang up the
Robinsons who live in Brighton.   9 She took
Margaret Thatcher off./She took off Margaret
Thatcher.   10 She took off Margaret Thatcher
making a speech.

15

1 with   2 into   3 off   4 into   5 into

16

1 turned   2 rush   3 landed   4 talked   5 reading

17

1 turned you off   2 land Polly with   3 rushed me
into   4 read more into   5 talked me into

18

1 up   2 on   3 down   4 up   5 with   6 on

19

1 bring   2 fix   3 put   4 took   5 make   6 put

20
1 put it down to   2 put him up to it   3 take her up on her offer   4 fix them up with   5 bring Tommy in on   6 make it up to you

21
1 run-through   2 check-up   3 mix-ups   4 fall-off   5 outlay   6 upkeep

22
1 check-ups   2 mix-up   3 hold-up   4 breakdown   5 run-through   6 break-ins

PART II

1   Putting things off
(Suggested answers)
I sometimes put off going to the doctor's/learning English vocabulary/taking an important decision. I often put off writing letters/paying bills/difficult work. I never put off going to the dentist's/doing homework/making an apology.

2   Things you couldn't do without
(Possible answers)
I couldn't do without my car because I go to work in it every day.
I couldn't do without my computer because it helps me to do my work very quickly.
I couldn't do without my typewriter because I need it for writing letters and reports.
I couldn't do without my English dictionary because I need it for writing essays.
I couldn't do without my tent because I like camping holidays.
I couldn't do without my video recorder because without it I would miss many interesting television programmes.
I couldn't do without my alarm-clock because I have to be at work/school early.
I couldn't do without my radio because I like to listen to music in my free time.
I couldn't do without my briefcase because I always have a lot of papers and books to carry.

3   Putting up with things
A
1 we had to put up with the smell of paint   2 we had to put up with noise and dirt   3 we had to put up with loud music at night   4 we had to put up with cold showers   5 we had to put up with slow service   6 we had to put up with a 4-hour delay

B (Suggested answers)
Factory workers usually have to put up with shift-work.
Nurses usually have to put up with long working hours and low pay.
Airline pilots usually have to put up with being away from home and working at weekends.
Workers on a building site usually have to put up with noise and dirt. They also have to put up with working outside in bad weather.
Taxi-drivers usually have to put up with irregular working hours and with working at weekends. Sometimes they have to put up with difficult customers.
Bus-drivers usually have to put up with working at weekends and with irregular working hours.
Postmen/postwomen usually have to put up with working outside in bad weather.
Waiters/waitresses usually have to put up with long working hours and with low pay. Sometimes they have to put up with difficult customers as well.

4   What could they do with?
A (Suggested answers)
1 She could do with a hot drink/a cup of tea/coffee.
2 The car could do with a new door/a new headlight/a few repairs.
3 He could do with a new suit/some new clothes.
4 She could do with some help/someone to help her.
5 His clothes could do with a wash.
6 He could do with a rest/a break.

B (Possible answers)
I could do with a new English dictionary because mine is not up to date/is old and torn/is not suitable for advanced students.
I could do with a book on English idioms because I want to learn how to use them/I want to improve my use of English.

I could do with a good night's sleep because I am
very tired today/I slept for only four hours last
night/I went to bed very late every night last week.
I could do with a long holiday because I have been
working very hard over the past weeks/I have been
ill.
I could do with a new car because mine has broken
down/can't be repaired/uses too much petrol/is ten
years old.
I could do with a new bicycle because mine is
broken/is very old/hasn't got any brakes/was stolen.

5   Looking things up
(Suggested answers)
1 I would look Chicago up on a map of North
   America/in an atlas.
2 I would look up the location of Trafalgar Square
   on a street map of London.
3 I would look up the arrival times of flights to
   London from Paris in a flight timetable.
4 I would look up the address of the London
   Tourist Board in a London telephone directory/in
   a guidebook of London.
5 I would look up the Grand Hotel, Brighton, in a
   hotel guide of England/Brighton.
6 I would look the word 'idiom' up in an English
   dictionary.
7 I would look George Stephenson up in an
   encyclopaedia.
8 I would look up a recipe for Yorkshire pudding in
   an English cookery book.
9 I would look up the location of the Victoria Falls
   on a map of Africa/in an atlas.
10 I would look up the times of trains from Oxford
   to London in a British Railways train timetable.

6   Getting on with people
(Possible answers)
I usually get on very well with my parents.
I usually get on quite well with my neighbours.
I don't get on at all well with my landlady.
I get on best with people who share my interests.
I get on best with people who are similar to me in
character and temperament.

7   Cutting down
(Suggested answers)
1 You can cut down on the cost of telephone calls by
   making calls as short as possible/by making calls at
   cheap-rate times.
2 You can cut down on electricity bills by turning
   down the heating/by turning off the television set
   (radio) when you are not really watching
   (listening)/by taking showers instead of baths/by
   using the dish-washer and washing-machine only
   when they are full.
3 You can cut down on personal spending by buying
   fewer clothes/by eating out only on special
   occasions/by taking cheaper holidays than usual/by
   walking or cycling instead of buying petrol/by
   giving presents that you can make yourself.

8   I've run out!
(Possible answers)
The worst time to run out of toothpaste is in the
early morning/when you are getting ready to go to
work/school.
The worst time to run out of coffee is when you are
expecting guests/when friends are coming to see
you/at breakfast time before the shops open.
The worst time to run out of eggs is when you want
to bake a cake/make pancakes/make an English
breakfast.
The worst time to run out of washing powder is
when you want to wash some clothes that you need
urgently/when you have a washing-machine full of
clothes.
The worst time to run out of writing paper is when
you have an urgent letter to write/when you are in
the middle of writing a letter or report.
The worst time to run out of stamps is when you
have an important letter to post/when the post office
is closed.
The worst time to run out of petrol is when you are a
long way from a petrol station/when you are driving
on a lonely road.
The worst time to run out of ideas is when you are
doing an examination/when you are writing an essay
in class/when you have a problem to solve in your
work.

The worst time to run out of money is when you are alone away from home/in a foreign country/not at home and feeling hungry/when you see a bargain in a shop window.

9   Finding out

A (Suggested answers)

1 A spy tries to find out the secrets of other countries.
2 A private detective tries to find out information about a certain person.
3 A doctor tries to find out what is wrong with a sick person.
4 A newspaper reporter tries to find out news about people and events.
5 A market researcher tries to find out which goods people want to buy and why.
6 A car mechanic tries to find out what is wrong with a car that has broken down.
7 A vet tries to find out what is wrong with a sick animal.
8 A TV repairman tries to find out what is wrong with a broken television set.

B (Suggested answers)

1 I would find out the price of a watch in a shop window by going into the shop and asking.
2 I would find out when the last bus goes home by asking a bus-driver/by looking in a bus timetable.
3 I would find out the exchange rate of the US dollar by asking at my bank/by looking in a daily newspaper.
4 I would find out whether someone is telling the truth by asking other people for the facts.
5 I would find out my neighbour's telephone number by looking in a telephone directory/ asking him or her.
6 I would find out how to make pizza by looking in a recipe book of Italian food.
7 I would find out how to play chess by asking someone who knows/by borrowing a book on chess from the library.
8 I would find out how much money I have in my bank account by looking at my last bank statement/by phoning the bank and asking.

10   Giving it up

(Possible answers)

I could easily give up going to parties/beer/cigarettes.
I couldn't give up smoking/playing football/watching television.
I wouldn't like to give up eating sweet things/my hobby/my daily work-out.

11   Flying made easy

Why get on, take off, drop off, wake up, get off, get on, take off, drop off, wake up and get off, when you could get on, take off, drop off, sleep, sleep, sleep, sleep, sleep, wake up and get off?

12   Talking about yourself

A (Possible answers)

1 I grew up in a small village.
2 My parents brought me up.
3 I take after my father. I take after him in looks./I take after my mother. I take after her in temperament.
4 I would like to settle down in my own country.
5 Yes, I am likely to go into teaching./No, I am likely to go into show business.

Test exercise 1

1 find out   2 took off   3 put it off   4 run out of
5 go into   6 grew up   7 takes after   8 settle down
9 cutting down on   10 get on with   11 do with
12 get off   13 put up with   14 brought him up
15 woke up   16 look it up   17 dropped off   18 do without it   19 get on   20 give it up

13   Puzzle: who's going where?

Peter is going on a camping holiday. Lucy is flying to Australia. Diana is going on a package holiday to Tenerife. Bill is flying to Greece on a study trip. Mike is touring Scotland by car.

14   Similar pairs (1)

1 get round him   2 get through it   3 get him round   4 get it over   5 get it through

15   Similar pairs (2)

A (Possible answers)

1 Mike was very helpful and charming to me this

morning. But I saw through him! He wanted to borrow some money.

2 At first the guard dog seemed quite friendly. But when I tried to get past him he turned on me.

3 'I've got a message for Susan from Robert. Will you give it to her, please?' 'All right. I'll pass it on.'

4 Try not to worry. If you need money or help, tell me. I'll see you through.

5 'I've just bought Michael Star's new album.' 'Can I borrow it? I love his music. It really turns me on!'

16   If I were prime minister . . .
A (Possible answers)
If I were prime minister I would clamp down on terrorists/put up more hospitals and universities/ bring down food prices/shut down nuclear power stations/bring in laws against drug-dealing/try to stamp out racial violence/shut down unprofitable industries/bring in stricter traffic laws/clamp down on environmental pollution/bring down government spending, etc.

17   Puzzle: a round-table discussion
Smith, Jones, Brown, Walker, Hill, Evans (clockwise)
1 Walker is sitting between Hill and Brown.
2 Brown likes to talk the others down.
3 Hill just looks on.
4 Walker keeps bringing up unimportant matters.
5 Hill is sitting opposite the man who keeps breaking in.

Test exercise 2
1 put up   2 get round her   3 checked in   4 bring it up   5 looking on   6 break in   7 pass it on   8 go off it   9 brush up on   10 get over it   11 see through her   12 shut down   13 bring in   14 stop over   15 get it over   16 nodding off   17 get through it   18 turn on me   19 come up with   20 putting up

18   Helping people
(Suggested answers)
1 I could go over it with him/her.
2 I would try to bring her round.
3 I would offer to pick them up.

4 I could try to call on him/her.
5 I could drop them off.
6 I would try to break it up.

19   What needs doing?
A
1 The old house needs doing up.
2 The garden shed needs clearing out.
3 The study needs tidying up.
4 The paintwork needs touching up.
5 The new fence needs finishing off.
6 The old silver candlestick needs cleaning up.

B (Suggested answers)
My bedroom needs tidying up. My writing-desk needs tidying up. My cupboards need clearing out. My drawers need clearing out. My car needs touching up. My bicycle needs cleaning up. My homework needs finishing off. My essay needs finishing off. My old books need sorting out. My old newspapers need sorting out. My photographs need sorting out. My letters need sorting out. Our house needs doing up. Our kitchen needs touching up. Our garage needs clearing out. Our attic needs clearing out.

20   What happened?
(Possible answer)
The delivery van drove off. The sportscar was behind the delivery van. The driver of the sportscar was impatient because the van was holding him up. The driver of the sportscar pulled out to overtake the van and speeded up. The sportscar was going to turn off, but at the junction the traffic lights were red. The sportscar cut in in front of the van and had to brake suddenly. The delivery van couldn't stop and ran into the back of the sportscar.

21   The law and you
1 slipped out/made off/ran off   2 come out   3 end up   4 run off/slip out/make off   5 makes off   6 pay up

22   Morning routine
1 He sets off from home at 7.45.   2 He usually stops off at the newsagent's/to buy a newspaper.   3 On

Sundays he lies in (until 9.30).   4 Jeff wakes up at 7.45.   5 His mother gets him up at 8 o'clock.   6 He sets off for school at 8.30.   7 On the way to school he picks up a friend.

Test exercise 3
1 turned off   2 bring her round   3 clearing it out
4 call on   5 cut in/pulled out   6 put me up   7 sort out   8 pick you up   9 go over it   10 drop them off   11 held me up   12 get up   13 end up   14 slip out   15 set off   16 lie in   17 finished off
18 speed up   19 made off   20 pull out

23   Doing puzzles (1)
1 read through   2 think about   3 work out   4 give up   5 look out for   6 catch you out   7 work out
8 come across   9 move on

24   Doing puzzles (2)
1 work out   2 mixed up, sort out, find out   3 work out   4 fit in with   5 filling in/working out   6 mixed up, sort them out, fit in with   7 work out   8 filling in/working out   9 fit them in   10 sort them out
Answers to puzzles: Example: orange, planet, twenty
1 two days   2 The Old Man and the Sea, Murder is Easy, The Thirty-nine Steps   3 six matches
4 figure d because the feet are pointing in the opposite direction   5 a 35, b 40   6 Greece, Italy, England, India, France. India does not fit in with the others, which are all countries of Europe.   7 bit, pet, pen   8 a K, b C   9 (top line) 4, 2; (bottom line) 8, 6
10 5, 1, 4, 3, 2

25   Check your health habits!
(Suggested answers)
I would do without sweet things. I would stick to health foods. I would work off surplus weight. I would do without meat. I would cut out salt. I would cut down on fat and sugar. I would do without strong coffee. I would cut down on carbohydrates. I would take up fitness training. I would stick to fish and vegetables. I would cut out fried foods. I would give up smoking. I would give up alcohol. I would stick to salads. I would cut down on chocolate. I would cut out Coca-Cola. I would work out every day.

26   Cartoon humour
1D, 2F, 3A, 4E, 5B, 6C

27   People and their jobs
(Possible answers)
A teacher usually likes dealing with children/is usually good at looking after children/is usually good at putting explanations across.
A door-to-door salesman is usually good at talking people into buying things.
A psychoanalyst is usually good at drawing people out/is usually good at dealing with people.
A travel courier usually likes getting about/dealing with people.
A zoo-keeper is usually good at looking after animals/usually likes dealing with animals.
A novelist is usually good at making up stories/ putting ideas and information across.
A journalist is usually good at finding out news about people, places and events/is usually good at putting information across.
A police detective is usually good at finding out information about people.
A fashion model usually likes dressing up and getting about.

28   Renting a car in the UK
1 take out   2 go about   3 back-up   4 breakdown
5 pick up   6 end up   7 drive off   8 drop it off

Test exercise 4
1 cut out   2 catch me out   3 taken up   4 fill them in   5 get about   6 work out   7 made it up   8 look after   9 talk you into it   10 mixed up   11 look out for   12 turn it off   13 stick to it   14 work off
15 come across it   16 worked it out   17 kept up
18 go about it   19 putting them across   20 deal with it.

29   Ringing people up
A (Possible answers)
1 Ann: Hello, Bill. This is Ann. I've tried to phone you three times, but I couldn't get through. I need some information about the new project.
   Bill: I haven't got all the information yet, so I'll get back to you later.

2 Mr Fox: Good morning, could you put me through to the bank manager, please?
Bank clerk: The manager will be free in a moment, Mr Fox, if you'd like to hold on.
3 Janet: Of course I'd like to come to the party.
Peter: Oh, I'll have to hang up, there's someone at the door. Sorry.
Janet: That's all right. Can you ring back later?
4 Mark: Hello, it's me again, Mark. We were cut off.
Kate: Oh, I thought you had hung up for some reason.
5 Andy: Can you give me Robert's address, Terry?
Terry: Yes, of course. Can you hold on until I get my address book? . . . I'm sorry, but I can't find it. I'll get back to you later.
Andy: That's all right. I have to hang up now anyway. I'm going out.

B (Possible answer)
A: Hello, this is A speaking. I tried to phone you yesterday, but I couldn't get through. Your number was engaged. Would you like to go to a jazz concert on the 17th?
B: Oh, that's a lovely idea, but I may have other plans for the 17th. If you hold on, I'll look in my diary.
A: Oh, there's someone at the door. I'll have to hang up now.
B: That's all right. I'll ring you back later.

30 Hit parade
1 Don't let me down. 2 We'll work it out. 3 I'll see you through. 4 If you stand by me. 5 Let's think it over. 6 You can always count on me.
7 Since you walked out on me. 8 But you were only leading me on. 9 I just can't do without her.
10 You're getting to me.

31 A problem shared
1 put in for, turned down, bring the matter up, see into it, have it out, go about it, talked me into staying, look up to me, get on with them, is getting me down, can't put up with it
2 applied for/requested, rejected, mention the matter, examine it, argue it to the end, approach it,

persuaded me to stay, respect me, have a good relationship with them, is depressing me, can't tolerate it

32 Telephone messages
A
1 do without it 2 pick me up 3 take you up on it 4 put you up 5 take me on 6 see him off 7 kept/keeps me up 8 ask you out 9 count on you 10 call for you/pick you up

B (Possible answers)
1 Bob rang up. He said he can't do without his pocket calculator.
2 Barbara rang up. She wants me to pick her up this afternoon.
3 Mike rang up. I offered him some free tickets for the football match. He wants to take me up on my offer.
4 Tom rang up. He said he and Jenny can easily put me up when I'm in Bristol.
5 John rang up. He said they are going to take him on at the research laboratory where he applied for a job.
6 Jim rang up. He asked me if I would like to go with him to the airport to see Dad off.
7 My neighbour from the flat below rang up. He complained that my loud music keeps/kept him up half the night.
8 Liz rang up. She wants to ask me out in return for a favour I did her.
9 Sue rang up. She wants to know if she can count on me to help with the party arrangements on Friday.
10 Jeff rang up. We're going to a jazz concert tonight. He will call for me/pick me up at seven-thirty.

33 Role reversal: stay-at-home fathers
1 bringing up 2 stand up to 3 gave up 4 look after 5 get on with 6 looks after 7 looking after 8 help out 9 carried on 10 cope with 11 turned out 12 carrying on 13 were up against 14 gave up 15 carried on 16 brought up

34   Do you work for a jerk?

1 bottling up   2 come across   3 find out   4 bring up   5 go over   6 deal with   7 wind up   8 carried away   9 dealing with   10 breaks down   11 bring up   12 deal with   13 putting off   14 going on

35   When would you say that?

(Possible answers)

1 A: If your headache's better, we could play tennis this afternoon.
   B: Sorry, I don't feel up to it.
2 A: I'm feeling very depressed because I failed the examination.
   B: Don't worry. You'll get over it.
3 A: I don't think the teacher believed your story, but if he asks you again, you mustn't change it.
   B: Whatever happens, I'm going to stick to it.
4 A: It's late. I really must go now.
   B: All right. I'll see you out.
5 A: I've passed my driving test at last!
   B: Congratulations! That calls for a celebration.
6 A: My boss has asked me if I'd like to go with him to Japan. Shall I go or not? What would you do?
   B: That's easy. I would jump at the chance.
7 A: We've found a lovely old house in the country. It's just what we want, so we're going to buy it.
   B: Take my advice. Don't rush into it.
8 A: I'd like the report on my desk to be typed as soon as possible, please.
   B: I'll see to it immediately.
9 A: I've bought my sister an Elton John LP for her birthday, but please don't tell her.
   B: All right. I promise I won't let on.
10 A: If you buy this car, I promise you won't regret it.
   B: I'll think it over.

Test exercise 5

1 think it over   2 hung up   3 feel up to it   4 turned out   5 carry on   6 cropped up   7 cope with them   8 take me on   9 get through   10 hold on   11 let him down   12 walk out on   13 get her down   14 turn down   15 call it off   16 see you off   17 look up to her   18 call for you   19 counting on me   20 take her up on it

36   Study habits

(Possible answers)

1 If I fall behind with my work, I try to catch up as soon as possible.
2 If I come across an English word that I don't understand I look it up in an English dictionary.
3 I look up new words and write them down. Then I go over them several times.
4 Yes, I have come across a few new words today.
5 Sometimes I give up easily, but usually I try to keep at it until I know how to do it.
6 I try to settle down to homework straightaway, but it's not always possible. I try to get on with it as soon as I can. Sometimes I put off doing it.
7 If I have a long exercise to do, I try to keep at it until it's finished, but sometimes I take a break.
8 When I have finished off an exercise, I usually go over it and look for mistakes.
9 If my homework was only half done, I would finish it off before my next lesson.
10 If I find an exercise difficult, I usually ask my teacher or a friend to go over it with me.

37   Ask Maggie!

A

1 False   2 True   3 False   4 True   5 False
6 True   7 True   8 False   9 True   10 True
11 False   12 True

38   Profile of Bruce Springsteen

A

1 grew up   2 give them up   3 get on with   4 drew up   5 signed up   6 broke up   7 called up   8 breakthrough   9 sell-out   10 given away   11 gave it all up   12 turned out   13 keep on

B (Possible answers)

Where did you grow up? The group once broke up. When did it break up and why? When did the record company sign you up? Have you ever wanted to give up singing? When did the big breakthrough come? Are all your concerts sell-outs?

39   Situations
(Possible answers)
1 I would send for a doctor.   2 I would own up (to my mistake).   3 I would think the offer over, but I would probably turn it down.   4 I would probably pick it/the £5 note up.   5 I would join in.
6 I would move out.   7 I would take my friend up on it/the offer.   8 I would jump at the chance./I would think it over./I would probably have to turn it down.   9 I would look him/her/my friend up.
10 I would call it/the barbecue off.

40   Giving up smoking
1 giving up/packing in   2 giving up/packing in
3 giving them away   4 take up   5 cutting down on
6 run out of   7 get up   8 washing-up   9 take up
10 give up   11 giving up/packing in   12 *Packing it in*   13 give it up/pack it in   14 fall into   15 lights up   16 settling down to   17 calms him down
18 get on with it

41   How self-confident are you?
(Possible answers)
 1 I sometimes stick up for myself.
 2 I almost always get on well with strangers.
 3 I rarely break in at meetings or discussions.
 4 I would rarely tell anyone to push off.
 5 I would rarely call on anyone I hardly know.
 6 I almost always blow up when I'm angry.
 7 I almost always answer back when someone is rude.
 8 I never brush a compliment aside.
 9 I sometimes go along with other people's suggestions.
10 I rarely sit out while others enjoy themselves.
11 I never give up easily when I feel challenged.
12 It sometimes takes me a long time to warm up.
13 I almost always let others push in.
14 I sometimes try to get out of doing things that make me the centre of attention.

Rating:
If your score is 14 to 20, you are bursting with self-confidence. You can handle any situation.
If your score is 21 to 30, you are reasonably self-confident, but learn to put yourself first more often.
If your score is 31 to 42, you tend to be shy at times.

Don't let the opinion of others influence you too much.
If your score is 43 to 56 you are extremely shy and should try to build up your self-confidence.

Test exercise 6
1 give up   2 fallen behind   3 settle down   4 push in   5 talk me round   6 fell for   7 taken in
8 keeps on   9 getting at me   10 keep at it   11 pack it in   12 get on with   13 look us up   14 get out of it   15 owned up   16 stuck up for him   17 go along with it   18 join in   19 brushed it aside   20 catch up with

42   Friends
1 No, a good friend doesn't lead you on.   2 No, a good friend doesn't hold out on you.   3 Yes, a good friend stands by you.   4 No, a good friend doesn't look down on you.   5 No, a good friend doesn't play up to you.   6 No, a good friend doesn't set you up.
7 Yes, a good friend stands up for you.   8 No, a good friend doesn't turn on you.   9 No, a good friend doesn't pick on you.   10 Yes, a good friend sees you through.

43   Talking about sport
1 get up to, go in for, keep it up, opt out, come up against, go through with, doing without, build up, stick to, give up, work out, pays off, settle for, look on
2 reach, participate in, continue it regularly, choose not to continue, are confronted with, complete/continue . . . to the end, not having/managing without, develop/increase, persevere with, stop eating, do physical fitness training, proves to be profitable, prepare to accept, watch inactively

44   On the road
A
1 backing out   2 driving off/pulling out   3 holding up
4 run into   5 broken down   6 pulled up/drawn up
7 cut in   8 turning off   9 slow down

B
1 cut out   2 broken down   3 change down
4 speed up   5 draw up

45   A true story
A
1 up   2 on   3 through   4 off   5 out   6 in
7 carried/went   8 without   9 on   10 up   11 out
12 broke   13 rolling   14 called   15 in   16 in

B
1 Her troubles began when her marriage broke up.
2 The money stopped coming in when her husband walked out.
3 No, she couldn't adapt to the change. She carried on buying nice things.
4 No, she also thought of her daughter. She didn't want her to go without the things she had been used to.
5 She ended up cleaning for a businessman.
6 She spotted some cheques made out to her boss's son.
7 She changed the name and paid them into her own account.
8 She broke down.
9 No, she couldn't take in what was happening to her.
10 She says she gave in to temptation.

Test exercise 7
1 pay off   2 call in   3 gave in to   4 going on
5 drawn up   6 take it in   7 look down on   8 stood up for him   9 come up against   10 slow down
11 settled for   12 broken down   13 made out
14 broke up   15 picks on

46   A life in the day of Celia Hammond
A
1 set   2 wake   3 find   4 on   5 put   6 tucking
7 up   8 turn   9 off   10 given   11 took   12 up
13 with   14 hanging   15 run   16 off

B
1 True   2 False   3 False   4 False   5 True
6 True   7 False   8 False   9 False   10 False

47   Your horoscope
A
1 True   2 True   3 False   4 True   5 False
6 True   7 False   8 True   9 True   10 True
11 False   12 True   13 True   14 True   15 True
16 False   17 False   18 True

48   How impulsive are you?
Rating:
If your score is 35 to 50 you are impulsive and relaxed. You live for the moment and rarely plan ahead. Life is a lot of fun, but it is also unpredictable. More control over your easy-going approach to life would help you to avoid future mistakes.

If your score is 20 to 35 you know where you are going in life, but you have not planned every step of the way. You are sometimes impulsive, but always flexible.

If your score is 10 to 20 you lack the impulsiveness that makes life fun. You like routine and are in control of all your actions. Stop planning so much. Relax more and just learn how to *be*.

Test exercise 8
1 try it on   2 came on   3 take it on   4 turn up
5 ring off   6 ring back   7 put it aside   8 dropping in on her   9 sat up   10 put you off it   11 settled on   12 drop by   13 set to   14 fall in with
15 come off

Index